BELIEVER'S HANDBOOK OF BATTLE STRATEGIES

A Bible-Based Approach to Spiritual Warfare

JOHN MARINELLI

TABLE OF CONTENTS

Preface v

Author's Note vii

Introduction ix

Part I ... The Battle of The Ages 1

Part II ...The Believer's Authority 40

Part III...Battle Strategies 63

Part IV Having Dominion 104

Conclusion 108

Selected Christian Poetry

By John Marinelli, The Author 109

About The Author 133

PREFACE

This book is designed as a Handbook for Christians that desire to learn scripture in an effort to overcome the attacks of the devil. We will look at several scripture passages and suggest how they can be used in daily living to deliver our souls from being captured and tormented by evil forces.

Walking in the Spirit is accomplished by the application of Bible truths. When we pray to be filled, God will usually lead us to His Word where we will discover great and powerful truths that can be applied to our daily life. As we apply them, we begin to walk in them and are translated into a perspective that is saturated with Faith.

This process is what I call, *"The Butterfly Effect."* We are like caterpillars crawling ever so slowly through life until we experience a transformation that changes us into a totally new creature, a butterfly. The caterpillar spent his days in fear, confusion, and other negative thoughts. But, the butterfly glides on the currents of the wind above the trials of life. It's a perfect word picture of the, "Born Again" experience.

AUTHOR'S NOTE

"Life and happiness are a perspective that can be attained, no matter what is going on around you. It all depends on how you look at life and how you apply God's Word to any given situation."

INTRODUCTION

The greatest battle of all times is the battle for the souls of mankind. It is a life and death struggle for every human being. It crosses ethnic groups, geographical boarders, social status, and all other lines that segment people into different levels. No one is exempt. We are all targets for the enemy of God.

If you think this is not true, read **I Peter 5:8-9** "Be sober, be vigilant; because your adversary the devil, as a roaring lion, walks about, seeking whom he may devour: Whom resist steadfast in the faith, knowing that the same afflictions are accomplished in your brethren that are in the world."

I want to expose our enemy and his tricks so you do not fall prey to his dominance and subsequent control. We will be looking at God's original plan for man and how Satan destroyed it. We will also be looking at God's provision for man after he lost his way.

The King James Version of the Bible will be the main source for knowledge and revelation as it is the inspired Word of God, written for our edification. "All scripture is given by inspiration of God, and is profitable for doctrine, for reproof, for correction, for instruction in righteousness:" **II Timothy 3:16**

PART I ... THE BATTLE OF THE AGES

I will mix bible truth, personal experience and comments from noteworthy individuals in an effort to explain,"The Battle of the Ages" which has been going on since the human race came into existance. The war is between God and His enemies over the souls of mankind.

My purpose is to enlighten the reader as to the battle, the enemy and the strategies use to capture and/or destroy the human soul. I also have specific goals that I will hopefully attain. They are as follows:

1. To bring to light the weapons of our warfare.

2. To educate on how to use these weapons.

3. To reveal specific Godly strategies that always win.

4. To provide a clear rationale for why such a battle exists, how it came to be and its ultimate end.

5. To establish a foundation from which a believer can build a life and destiny through God.

The Enemy of Our Souls

Peter describes our enemy as, ***"your adversary the devil"*** as he writes his second letter to various churches in Asia Minor sometime between 64 AD and 68 AD. He does not say Nero or the Romans in general are their enemy. Instead, he points his finger directly at the devil and tells them that this evil entity is their adversary.

An adversary, according to the dictionary is, "a person, group, or force that opposes or attacks; opponent; enemy; foe."

The bible calls Satan by many different names, including the devil, but he is still the same sinister opponent that we have to face in battle every day. Here's a list for your review:

Accuser

"Then I heard a loud voice saying in heaven, 'Now salvation, and strength, and the kingdom of our God, and the power of His Christ have come, for the ***accuser of our brethren***, who accused them before our God day and night, has been cast down.'" **Revelation 12:10**

Adversary

"Be sober, be vigilant; because your adversary the devil walks about like a roaring lion, seeking whom he may devour." **1 Peter 5:8**

Angel of light

"And no wonder! For Satan himself transforms himself into an angel of light." II **Corinthians 11:14**

Antichrist

"And every spirit that does not confess that Jesus Christ has come in the flesh is not of God. And this is the spirit of the Antichrist, which you have heard was coming, and is now already in the world." **1 John 4:3**

Beelzebub

"Now when the Pharisees heard it they said, 'this fellow does not cast out demons except by Beelzebub, the ruler of the demons.'" **Matthew 12:24**

Belial

"And what accord has Christ with Belial? Or what part has a believer with an unbeliever?" II **Corinthians 6:15**

Deceiver

"So the great dragon was cast out, that serpent of old, called the devil and Satan, who deceives the whole world; he was cast to the earth, and his angels were cast out with him." **Revelation 12:9**

Devil

"He who sins is of the devil, for the devil has sinned from the beginning. For this purpose the Son of God was manifested, that He might destroy the works of the devil." **1 John 3:8**

Dragon

"So the great dragon was cast out, that serpent of old, called the Devil and Satan, who deceives the whole world; he was cast to the earth, and his angels were cast out with him**." Revelation 12:9**

Enemy

"The enemy who sowed them is the devil, the harvest is the end of the age, and the reapers are the angels." **Matthew 13:39**

Evil One

"I do not pray that You should take them out of the world, but that You should keep them from the evil one." **John 17:15**

Father of Lies

"You are of your father the devil, and the desires of your father you want to do. He was a murderer from the beginning, and does not stand in the truth, because there is no truth in him. When he speaks a lie, he speaks from his own resources, for he is a liar and the father of it." **John 8:44**

God of This World

"Whose minds the God of this world has blinded, who do not believe, lest the light of the gospel of the glory of Christ, who is the image of God, should shine on them." **2 Corinthians 4:4**

Lawless One

"8. And then the lawless one will be revealed, whom the Lord will consume with the breath of His mouth and destroy with the brightness of His coming. 9. The coming of the lawless one is according to the working of Satan, with all power, signs, and lying wonders, 10. and with all unrighteous deception among those who perish, because they did not receive the love of the truth, that they might be saved." II **Thessalonians 2:8-10**

Leviathan

"In that day the LORD with His severe sword, great and strong, Will punish Leviathan the fleeing serpent, Leviathan that twisted serpent; And He will slay the reptile that is in the sea." **Isaiah 27:1**

Liar

"You are of your father the devil, and the desires of your father you want to do. He was a murderer from the beginning, and does not stand in the truth, because there is no truth in him. When he speaks a lie, he speaks from his own resources, for he is a liar and the father of it." **John 8:44**

Lucifer

"12. How you are fallen from heaven, O Lucifer, son of the morning!

How you are cut down to the ground, You who weakened the nations!

13. For you have said in your heart: 'I will ascend into heaven, I will exalt my throne above the stars of God; I will also sit on the mount of the congregation on the farthest sides of the north; 14. I will ascend above the heights of the clouds, I will be like the Most High.'" **Isaiah 14:12-14**

Man of Sin

"3. Let no one deceive you by any means; for that Day will not come unless the falling away comes first, and the man of sin is revealed, the son of perdition, 4. who opposes and exalts himself above all that is called God or that is worshiped, so that he sits as God in the temple of God, showing himself that he is God." **2 Thessalonians 2:3,4**

Murderer

"44. You are of your father the devil, and the desires of your father you want to do. He was a murderer from the beginning, and does not stand in the truth, because there is no truth in him. When he speaks a lie, he speaks from his own resources, for he is a liar and the father of it." **John 8:44**

Prince of The Power of The Air

"1. And you He made alive, who were dead in trespasses and sins, 2. in which you once walked according to the course of this world, according to the prince of the power of the air, the spirit who now works in the sons of disobedience." **Ephesians 2:1,2**

Roaring Lion

"Be sober, be vigilant; because your adversary the devil walks about like a roaring lion, seeking whom he may devour." **1 Peter 5:8**

Rulers of The Darkness

"For we do not wrestle against flesh and blood, but against principalities, against powers, against the rulers of the darkness of this age, against spiritual hosts of wickedness in the heavenly places." **Ephesians 6:12**

Ruler of This World

"31. Now is the judgment of this world; now the ruler of this world will be cast out. 32. And I, if I am lifted up from the earth, will draw all peoples to myself." **John 12:31,32**

Satan

"And He was there in the wilderness forty days, tempted by Satan, and was with the wild beasts; and the angels ministered to Him." **Mark 1:13**

Serpent of Old

"So the great dragon was cast out, that serpent of old, called the Devil and Satan, who deceives the whole world; he was cast to the earth, and his angels were cast out with him." **Revelation 12:9**

Son of Perdition

"3. Let no one deceive you by any means; for that Day will not come unless the falling away comes first, and the man of sin is revealed, the son of perdition, 4. who opposes and exalts himself above all that is called God or that is worshiped, so that he sits as God in the temple of God, showing himself that he is God." **2 Thessalonians 2:3,4**

Tempter

"Now when the tempter came to Him, he said, 'If You are the Son of God, command that these stones become bread.'" **Matthew 4:3**

Thief

"The thief does not come except to steal, and to kill, and to destroy. I have come that they may have life, and that they may have it more abundantly." **John 10:10**

Wicked One

"Above all, taking the shield of faith with which you will be able to quench all the fiery darts of the wicked one." **Ephesians 6:16**

This list of names for Satan has been taken from the New King James Version of the Bible.

There may be other names for Satan in the Bible. This is a partial list on the Internet developed by Nora Roth, a bible student. I offer her list because it is very accurate.

It should be evident by now, from all the names, that our enemy is bent on killing us or at best, keeping us from learning the truth about God and His love. These names form a portrait of evil. However, they also reveal how Satan operates.

It's like we have been given the playbook of the opposing team so we can learn their plays and develop a defense against them. Here's what we face:

1. We will have to deal with lies that are made against us.

2. We will be accused day and night by evil forces that watch our every move.

3. We will be tempted with stuff that appeals to our own lust and fallen nature.

4. We will be fighting deception on every hand.

5. We will see the truth becomes a lie and the lie accepted as truth in our society.

6. We will have to guard our hearts and protect our stuff against a masterful thief that stalks us day and night.

7. We will have to exercise a lot of faith to keep from being hurt by "fiery darts" being hurled by the Wicked One.

8. We will have to wrestle against principalities, against powers, against the rulers of the darkness of this age, against spiritual hosts of wickedness in the heavenly places who are bent on our destruction.

The Devil's Crowd

It is true that our battle is with demons who are spiritual beings bent on our destruction. However, the devil also works through people. I call them, "The Devil's Crowd" This group consists of folks that deny Jesus as coming in the flesh. They are those that the Bible calls, "Antichrists". They support abortion, same sex marriage, child pornography, wife swapping, and all the other liberal agenda currently being pushed in our society.

Sadly enough, these folks are in many instances, our parents, kids, neighbors, political officials and co-workers. Satan uses them to spread his Anti-Christ gospel message.

My wife, just for the fun of it, searched the Internet for crime in our area. She found all sorts of evil going, all within one mile from our home. Now that's scary. However, Satan will use any-one that is not on guard spiritually to attack another. He has a host of demons that do nothing but make suggestions to us to be a certain way or do inappropriate things from off-color jokes to hostile acts.

Evil Spirits To Watch For

People often reflect the evil spirit that controls them. Here are a few to watch for. You've seen them before but didn't know that they were evil spirits. We say, this person has a spirit of: Jealousy, Dominance, Suicide, Murder, Homosexuality, Criticism, Anger, and so forth.

I know that the deeds of the flesh portray the same things but when you see more than a passing attitude, you can rest assured that there is probably a demon behind it. They drive the individual to over react and display their own evil nature. It's how they live. It's through those who they control. The major sign that shows a demonic attachment is abnormality, Excessive or Extreme.

I guess it's clear that we are truly in a life and death battle and our eternal soul hangs in the balance.

The Battleground

The battleground, where all the fighting takes place, is in your mind. You may be on a playground, at work, with family or friends but victory or defeat is all about how you think. **Listen to what Paul told the early church.**

"And be not conformed to this world: but be ye transformed by the renewing of your mind, that ye may prove what is that good, and acceptable, and perfect, will of God." **Romans 12:2**

Here the voices of the Old Testament Prophets And New Testament Apostles

"And all this assembly shall know that the Lord saves not with sword and spear: *for the battle is the Lord's, and he will give you into our hands*." **1st Samuel 17:47**

"And it shall be, when thou shalt hear a sound of going in the tops of the mulberry trees, that then thou shalt go out to **battle**: *for God is gone forth before thee* to smite the host of the Philistines." **I Chronicles 14:15**

"Who is this King of glory? The Lord strong and mighty, *the Lord mighty in battle*." **Psalm 24:8**

"*Therefore he hath poured upon him the fury of his anger*, and the strength of **battle**: and it hath set him on fire round about, yet he knew not; and it burned him, yet he laid it not to heart." **Isaiah 42:25**

"*Thou art my battle axe and weapons of war*: for with thee will I break in pieces the nations, and with thee will I destroy kingdoms;" **Jeremiah 51:20**

There is some good news so don't get too depressed.

First, *The battle is the Lords*. " Thus saith the Lord unto you, be not afraid nor dismayed by reason of this great multitude; for the battle is not yours, but God's." **II Chronicles 20:15** God wants us to know that He has everything under control.

Second, *God has given us His amour to wear so we don't get hurt*. "Finally, my brethren, be strong in the Lord, and in the power of his might. Put on the whole armor of God, that ye may be able to stand against the wiles of the devil. For we wrestle not against flesh and blood, but against principalities, against powers, against the rulers of the darkness of this world, against spiritual wickedness in high places. ...**Ephesians 6:10-18**

Third, *Jesus has already defeated every evil power.* " And having despoiled principalities and powers, He made a show of them openly, triumphing over them in it.**" Colossians 2:15** The victory was at the cross where He died as a sacrifice for sin. "For what the law could not do, in that it was weak through the flesh, God sending his own Son in the likeness of sinful flesh, and for sin, condemned sin in the flesh:" **Romans 8:3**

Finally, *God wants us to walk in the Spirit so we do not fulfill the deeds of the flesh.* "This I say then, Walk in the Spirit, and ye shall not fulfill the lust of the flesh." **Galatians 5:16** The deeds of the flesh are listed in Galatians 5. It is the flesh that causes us all the problems.

Paul tells us in **Romans 8** that living in the flesh is to be carnally minded and that cannot be blessed of God or favored in any way. It brings only death to our souls. God is in the business of bringing life not death.

A sobering thought...this evil nature, (personality), that is seen in Satan, who is our mortal enemy, has somehow manifested itself in us. The deeds of the flesh are identical to the personality of the devil. How can this be? God did not create us this way.

The Creation of Man, His Fall And Restoration

"And God said, Let us make man in our image, after our likeness: and let them have dominion over the fish of the sea, and over the fowl of the air, and over the cattle, and over all the earth, and over every creeping thing that creeps upon the earth. So God created man in his own image, in the image of God created he him; male and female created he them. And God blessed them, and God said unto them, Be fruitful, and multiply, and replenish the earth, and subdue it: and have dominion over the fish of the sea, and over the fowl of the air, and over every living thing that moves upon the earth." **Genesis 1:26-28**

Note that God created man in His image and likeness. What do we know about the likeness and image of God? Only this…it is a Holy Image and a Righteous likeness. **(Galatians 5:22)** There is no sin in Him. Yet man is all of a sudden filled with another image…that of Satan. Paul tells us all about what really happened to Adam and how it affected our destiny.

"Wherefore, as by one man sin entered into the world, and death by sin; and so death passed upon all men, for that all have sinned:" **Romans 5:12**

Adam was a prototype, the 1st of many to come. However, with his disobedience came sin instead of Holiness. Instead of righteousness flowing from Adam to his descendants, sin overtook them all. Instead of the image of God remaining in Adam and being duplicated in his descendants, the nature and character of Satan filled the souls of man. Paul refers to Christ as the 2nd Adam. "And so it is written, the first man, Adam, was made a living soul; the last Adam *was made* a quickening spirit." **I Corinthians 15:45**

Some will disagree with me about Adam falling from God's grace and creating a world of sin. They will say that we are all children of God. However **Romans 8:14** tells us, "For as many as are led by the Spirit of God, they are the sons of God.

There is another logical argument for the fall of man. It is in Genesis. It would be wrong to say that God created man in His own image, verse 1:26, and that image was both good and evil. To say such a thing is to say that God is also the devil, which is ludicrous. God is pure and morally righteous. He does not change. There is no darkness in Him. That means that man had to change. He chose to disobey God and lost his innocence. Instead of God's image, he accepted the image of Satan.

Here's how that all happened, according to the bible. It's recorded in **Genesis Chapter three**, "Now the serpent was more crafty than any of the wild animals the Lord God had made. He said to the woman, "Did God really say, 'You must not eat from any tree in the garden'?" The woman said to the serpent, "We may eat fruit from the trees in the garden, but God did say, "you must not eat fruit from the tree that is in the middle of the garden, and you must not touch it, or you will die." "You will not certainly die," the serpent said to the woman. "For God knows that when you eat from it your eyes will be opened, and you will be like God, knowing good and evil."

Note the lie that Satan tells Eve. The lie is three-fold

1. "You will not surely die"

2. "You will be like God"

3. "You will know good and evil".

They were already like God, in that…they bore His image and likeness. They were not supposed to know evil. It was not in

God's plan for man. What really happened was they knew evil by nature but lost the ability to know good.

Death was swift and sure but not physical, only spiritual. Physical came later. The Spirit's breath put into Adam was taken away and therefore it could not pass on to his descendants. That's why the New Testament says we must be, "Born Again".

Satan always tells lies to deceive us. If we buy the lie, we live out that destiny. If, on the other hand, we know the truth, it will set us free to shape our own destiny in accordance with God's will.

Knowing the truth is the greatest weapon we can have and use against evil influences. If you are not sure of what is truth, read the Bible. It is full of God's Word. Here's an example of how to use it to defeat Satan.

The enemy says to you, in the form of a thought that pops into your head, "You can rob a store and get the needed cash to buy that thing you've always wanted" "If no one sees you, you're Scott Free" "That company is insured anyway and will not miss what you steal" A simple declaration of truth will dispel the lie and keep your mind in focus with God's Will. Here's the declaration, **"Thou Shalt not Steal".** The truth of God's Word will always dispel the lie and expose its source.

So Adam fell from God's grace when he disobeyed God. His transgression was so bad that God could not fix it without violating the free will to choose his/her own destiny. Adam chose to experience evil and he did...and so did we. However, there's always a, "But God" in every Divine story.

Man Is Restored By God

But God didn't leave Adam and Eve to a hell-bound destiny. He, from before the foundation of the world, had a plan to redeem His greatest creation. The apostle John records Jesus as He tells Nicodemus, a religious leader, the plan of redemption. **John 3:16** "For God so loved the world, that he gave his only begotten Son, that whosoever believeth in him should not perish, but have everlasting life."

It's important to note that salvation is available/given to every, **"Whosoever"** that believes. All that is necessary is to believe that God sent Jesus, His only Son to redeem mankind. Jesus is the only way to God and that is through the, "Born Again" experience.

"Only Way To God?"
True or False?

It is hard for most folks that are not "Born Again" to understand why there is just one way to God, yet it is true. There is only one way and that is through Jesus Christ. The Bible is our source to prove that the one-way doctrine is valid. **Acts 4:12** says, "Neither is there salvation in any other: for there is no other name under heaven given among men, whereby we must be saved."

Jesus is the only way to attain salvation. All the world religions cannot save us. Joining a church or specific faith cannot save us. It must be an acknowledgment of our sin, our cry before the throne of God for forgiveness, and our invitation for Jesus to come into our hearts and save us. His name is the only one that can get us through death into eternal life.

Here are a few scriptures that support the only "One-Way" doctrine.

1. ...There is one God, and one mediator between God and men, the man Christ Jesus; Who gave himself a ransom for all, to be testified in due time. **(I Timothy 2:5-6)**

2. ... Believe on the Lord Jesus Christ and thou shalt be saved... **(Acts 16:31)**

3. ...That if thou shalt confess with thy mouth the Lord Jesus, and shalt believe in thine heart that God hath raised him from the dead, THOU SHALT BE SAVED. For with the heart man believeth unto righteousness; and with the mouth confession is made unto salvation. **(Romans 10:9-10)**

The skeptic would say, "You mean to tell me that all the religions of the world are wrong and only Christianity is the one true religion?" Remember, Christianity is not a religion. It is a relationship born out of love between man and the one true and living God. There is no one true religion. Religion, in itself, will not get us to God. It is the blood of Christ that unlocks the door and our confession of faith in Jesus that makes it all happen. **(John 14:6)**

Why is Jesus the only way to God? ...Because God planned it that way. He set the penalty for sin, which was death. *The soul that sinneth, it shall die.* **(Ezekiel 18:20)** In fact, Jesus was the slain Lamb of God before the foundation of the world. **(Ephesians 1:3-7)**

Jesus Himself said, as recorded in **John 14:6**, "I am the way, the truth, and the life: No man cometh to the Father but by Me".

Christianity states that the God of the Bible is the only true God and salvation is only possible by accepting Jesus Christ, His only begotten Son as Savior and Lord. **II Corinthians 5:21** says, "For he hath made him to be sin for us, who knew no sin; that we might be made the righteousness of God in him."

God validated His Son as the only way in multiple ways so we could be assured that Jesus was indeed the only way to Him. Here are some to consider.

1. He claimed to be the only way as in John's record 14:6 says but validation came through miracles that proved He was who He claimed to be.

2. Eyewitnesses saw Jesus' miracles and validated them as authentic. Over 500 followers saw Jesus, after His resurrection, and watched Him ascend into heaven.

3. The prophets foretold of His coming, where He would be born, that He would be God in human flesh and lots more…all prophetic statements were realized in Jesus, even those like in Isaiah chapter 53 that were uttered hundreds of years before Jesus came.

4. God Himself validated Jesus as His sole pathway to Him. "While he was still speaking, behold, a bright cloud overshadowed them; and suddenly a voice came out of the cloud, saying, "This is my beloved Son, in whom I am well pleased. Hear ye Him!"(**Mathew 17:5**)

5. The Apostles lost their homes, wealth, and even their lives preaching the gospel. Would they do that if it were a lie? I don't think so. They testified to the truth

and were willing to die for it if necessary. **(See Foxes Book of Martyrs)**

6. Thousands of believers, over several centuries have testified of how Jesus helped them and blessed them.

7. I can personally testify that I have seen the hand of the Lord in my life and communicate with Him daily. I know He is the Christ.

The provability that one man could fulfill all prophecies about a Messiah that God Himself said would come, **(Gen. 3:15)**, and perform fantastic miracles while here on earth, and be raised from the dead, and ascend into heaven while hundreds looked on is astronomical. But Jesus did just that…fulfilled everything that was foretold about the coming Messiah. He had to be who He said He was and therefore is truly the only way to God.

Question: How does my salvation overcome the attacks of the devil? The answer is in the Bible. God is calling all of us to Himself so we can be set free from sin, death and the wilds of the devil. If we do not rely on Him, we are not blessed and protected.

Here's a scripture that explains it further. "The angel of the LORD encampeth round about them that fear him, and delivereth them." **Psalm 34:7** The key to being protected is to fear (Reverence) the Lord. When you do, His angel sets up his camp, that is filled with waring angels, all around you. Those that do not believe do not reverence and therefore do not qualify for The Angel of The Lord's Campfire.

You may be saying, "The bible is just a book and not a final authority. Let's look at this more closly.

The Bible As The Final Authority

I use the Bible as my main source to validate all that I say. But most people, including Christians, do not read the Bible with any regularity and therefore do not know the God of the Bible. They know only what their pastor or others tell them. Here's a brief history lesson.

The history of the Bible starts with a phenomenal account, the creation of all things. It's not one book like many think -- It's an ancient collection of writings, comprised of 66 separate books, written over approximately 1,600 years, by at least 40 distinct authors. The Old Testament contains 39 books written from approximately 1500 BC to 400 BC, and the New Testament contains 27 books written from approximately 40 to 90 AD. The Jewish Bible (*Tanakh*) is the same as the Christian Old Testament, except for its book arrangement. The original Old Testament was written mainly in Hebrew, with some Aramaic, while the original New Testament was written in common Greek.

Starting in about 40 AD, and continuing to about 90 AD, the eyewitnesses to the life of Jesus, including Matthew, Mark, Luke, John, Paul, James, Peter and Jude, wrote the Gospels and letters that eventually became the Bible's New Testament. These authors quote from 31 books of the Old Testament. They widely circulated their material so that by about 150 AD, early Christians were referring to the entire set of writings as the "New Covenant." During the 200s AD, the original writings were translated from Greek into Latin, Coptic (Egypt) and Syriac (Syria), and widely disseminated as "Inspired Scripture" throughout the Roman Empire and beyond. In 397 AD, in an effort to protect the scriptures from various heresies and offshoot religious movements, the current 27 books of the New Testament were formally and finally confirmed and "canonized" in the Synod of Carthage.

What I hope you will see from this snapshot of the Bible in history is that God took great pains to validate His Word to man over many years, keeping it clear, and indisputable as the only true source of His revelation. These eyewitness accounts and prophetic revelations all connect to make a complete proof of God's existence, character, power, love, salvation, judgment, compassion, mercy and forgiveness. His entire plan of salvation and the ages to come is all written down so we could benefit from them.

Time and time again I have asked the Lord questions and found the answers in the Bible. I can remember one in particular. I was attending a small Christian fellowship that met in a barn. The leadership was teaching that God's judgment upon America was to come soon and that they could escape it by leaving the states and going to a remote desert-like place in another country. Several families had already moved to this undisclosed location. I was a very young believer and not as knowledgeable as I am now in the scriptures...so I turned to Jesus and asked Him if these people were correct and if I should go with them. Here's what I read during my prayer and Bible reading.

Matthew 24:26 "Wherefore if they shall say unto you, Behold, he is in the desert; go not forth: behold, he is in the secret chambers; believe it not."

This is just one example of many that God has communicated to me through the Bible. Try it...when you are troubled, confused or worried about life or just need an answer to life's never ending questions, pray and ask Jesus to show you in His Word, the Bible.

The Bible was written under "Inspiration" from the Holy Spirit.

The word, "inspire" means "To breathe upon or into something". God revealed Himself through individuals who penned the written word.

As a young Christian, I often witnessed to un-believers, using the Bible as my source. Some of those I talked to told me that the Bible was not a source they would believe. I went to my pastor and asked him what I should do because folks were not open to hear what the Bible had to say. He led me to **Hebrews 4:12** and said. "Use it anyway," for the reasons stated in chapter four. Listen to what it says. "For the word of God is quick, and powerful, and sharper than any two-edged sword, piercing even to the dividing asunder of soul and spirit, and of the joints and marrow, and is a discerner of the thoughts and intents of the heart." **(Hebrews 4:12)** I did just that and began to see the words of the Bible break down barriers and soften hearts.

I know that anyone who is really seeking God and wants to know about Jesus will find everything in the Bible. Words will leap off the page, bringing fresh revelation, historical facts, wisdom, divine counsel and victory over life's every trial. All you have to do is spend some time every day in prayer and Bible reading.

Tricks of The Devil

Satan has many tricks and plays them on humans all the time. www.beliefnet.com offers several tricks or lies that are meant to capture your soul and leave you helplessly void of God's grace. I have chosen five to use in my book. Here they are:

1. That Happiness Is Unattainable

The devil wants you to stress about things you cannot control. He wants you confused, anxious, and even angry about your life circumstances so that you will eventually become distant from God, and rely on your own understanding.

2. That God's Word Isn't Real

The devil wants to trick you into believing the Bible is a collection of myths, in hopes that you will doubt God's Word and even His existence. He also wants you to believe that the Bible, written nearly 3500 years ago is no longer relevant in our modern world. But God's Word is real and has real significance. Not only was it written by more than 40 different writers over a 1600-year span with remarkable consistency, it explains life and the human experience in a way no other book has or ever will.

3. That You Aren't Significant

While God wants you to live a life filled with purpose, the devil wants the opposite. He doesn't want you to think or care about your thoughts, attitude, words or actions and will trick you into believing you aren't significant. If he gets you to believe your life is without purpose, then you will live a life of sin, out of tune with God. But your life is significant. God knew you before you were even born. Remember, He knows the plans He has for you, plans to prosper you and not to harm you; plans to give you hope and a future **(Jeremiah 29:11)**.

4. That Gossip Does No Harm, And Your Words Can't Hurt

The devil wants you to spread gossip and bad news so that you will focus on the negative and not believe in God's goodness or

His blessings. If he tricks you into thinking gossip does no harm, you will then believe there's nothing wrong in spreading harmful or malicious words which can hurt the people you love, and allow you to develop a negative view of the world around you, which has an impact on all that you do.

5. That The Physical World Outweighs The Spiritual World

If the devil can get you to believe that the physical world is more real than the <u>spiritual</u> world, he can trick you into pursuing things like money, power and fame and have you believing that materialistic things are more important than being in a relationship with God. If you think this, then you won't seek first the kingdom of God. But there is far more greatness in God's Heavenly Kingdom than any material possession we acquire while in physical form on Earth. Remember, Earth is now. Heaven is forever.

Weapons of Our Warfare

It's obvious that we need to know what our weapons are and how to use them…so lets look at some spiritual weapons. (For the weapons of our warfare *are* not carnal, but mighty through God to the pulling down of strong holds;) We will 1st look at the **Armor Of God** as presented in **Ephesians 6:13-17.**

"Therefore, take up the full armor of God, so that you will be able to resist in the evil day, and having done everything, to stand firm. Stand firm therefore, Having Girded Your Loins With Truth, and Having Put on the Breastplate of Righteousness, and having shod your Feet With The Preparation of the Gospel of Peace; in addition to all, taking up the shield of faith with which you will be able to extinguish all the flaming arrows of the *evil one*. And take the Helmet of Salvation, and the Sword of the Spirit, which is the Word of God."

So, we have Truth, Righteousness, Peace, Faith, Salvation and the Word of God or Bible…Six weapons, five defensive and one offensive. This represents the full armor of God to be worn and used so that we can resist evil.

Evil is the hour of temptation when Satan seeks to deceive us and draw us away from God. It is also when fiery darts are flung at us by demons. The deceptions are suggestive in nature that contradict God's will but seem logical such as, "everybody's do-ing it. Therefore it must be ok" or "drugs can't really hurt you." The fiery darts are insults like, "You're not good enough", "Not worth anything", "Never amount to anything"…all are negative in nature that are meant to cause a low self-esteem, depression and even suicide.

The Sword of the Spirit is really cool because it's fashioned from over 3,000 promises of God…things like; "You are accepted in the beloved" **Ephesians 1:6,** "I am crucified with Christ: never-theless I live; yet not I, but Christ lives in me: and the life which I now live in the flesh I live by the faith of the Son of God, who loved me, and gave himself for me." **Galatians 2:20,** "Nay, in all these things we are more than conquerors through him that loved us." **Romans 8:37**

All of Satan's efforts are designed to establish strongholds in our lives. How many has he established in you? What's a stronghold? Try these on for size: Over-eating, drugs, smoking, anger, homo-sexuality, pornography, and all of the deeds of the flesh listed in Galatians chapter five. He'll try and try until he gets you hooked on some sort of vice. If you follow him, he takes you deeper and deeper into it until a stronghold is built which is really an out-post for demonic activity. Not to worry because the Sword of the Spirit can cut that evil stronghold into pieces and bring its efforts to naught.

K. N. O. B. S.

As a young Christian, I learned an acrostic that helped me to re-member my primary weapons.

K = Knowledge Of God…" Casting down imaginations, and every high thing that exalteth itself against the knowledge of God, and bringing into captivity every thought to the obedience of Christ;" **II Corinthians 10:5**

Note: Anything that sets itself against what you know to be true, you cast it down and away from you.

N = Name Of Jesus… "That at the name of Jesus every knee should bow, of *things* in heaven, and *things* in earth, and *things* under the earth;" **Philippians 2:10**

Note: We can use our lord's name to stop the evil attack. Say it out loud if need be…"I cast you out and bind your influence from me, In The Name of Jesus, be gone.

O = Obedience… "And bringing into captivity every thought to the obedience of Christ;" **II Corinthians 10:5**

Note: we are to bring every thought into captivity. In other words…hold every thought against the truth of the Word of God to be sure it is not a deception or trap. Your obedience to the truth will keep you free.

B = Blood Of Christ …" If we confess our sins, he is faithful and just to forgive us *our* sins, and to cleanse us from all unrighteousness."

Note: through confession, His blood can cleanse us from our sin. That means when Satan accuses us, we can put it under the blood in confession before the throne of God and know it will fade away. Satan will try to use it anyway but we can stand against it, saying we've been forgiven.

S = Sword Of The Spirit... "For the word of God *is* quick, and powerful, and sharper than any two-edged sword, piercing even to the dividing asunder of soul and spirit, and of the joints and marrow, and *is* a discerner of the thoughts and intents of the heart." **Hebrews 4:12 Note:**

We can use the Word of God to fight back. It will always win.

Other "Word" Weapons

Consider these:

- **Give No Place To The Devil**..."Neither give place to the devil." **Ephesians 4:27**

Note: The best thing you can do is do not argue, negotiate, compromise or allow any negative or suggestive thoughts into your mind.

- **Prayer & Praise....** "Let God arise, let his enemies be scattered: let them also that hate him flee before him. ² As smoke is driven away, so drive them away: as wax melts before the fire, so let the wicked perish at the presence of God." **Psalm 68:1 & 2**

Note: Prayer always works as a weapon and when you add praise, you have a powerful combination that Satan cannot overcome.

- **Trust In The Lord At All Times**..."Trust in the LORD with all your heart and lean not on your own understanding; in all your ways submit to him, and he will make your paths straight." **Proverbs 3:5-6**

Note: Too many folks worry, cry and cuss over their circumstances. Learning to trust requires an absolute allegiance to Jesus, knowing He will direct you in and through every situation.

- **All Things Work Together For Good...**" And we know that all things work together for good to them that love God, to them who are the called according to his purpose." **Romans 8:28**

Note: Here's a great weapon because its foundation is the knowledge that God has a master plan and He is always working everything together for good in the lives of those who are called to salvation, all those, "Whosoevers" of **John 3:16** who love the Lord. If that is you, you can know that God is ever in your background, making things right.

- **Let The Peace of God Be The Referee**..."And let the peace of God rule in your hearts, to **the** which also ye are called in one body; and be ye thankful." **Colossians 3:16**

Note: If we can allow the peace of God to rule in our hearts, it will keep out all the clutter that Satan tries to fill our minds with. It's another great weapon in defensive warfare.

- **Stand Fast...**"Stand fast therefore in the liberty wherewith Christ hath made us free, and be not entangled again with the yoke of bondage" **Galatians 5:1**

Note: With all of the above weapons available to us, we should not fear Satan. He is a defeated foe. He has to steal your power to have any of his own. If we treat him accordingly, as a defeated foe, by standing fast to our confession of faith in Jesus and applying the scriptures against his attacks, we will no doubt remain peaceful, happy and free to serve our Lord.

I am sure that you'll find more weapons. Our salvation sets us free from the bondage of sin. Going back into that lifestyle is just not an option. We need to recognize the battle, learn about our enemy and use the weapon of choice to overcome the attack. Failing to fight is to lose it before you start and settle for a life in captivity.

Fighting Demonic Spirits

When we discuss fighting demonic spirits, it is easy to fall into error. One error is that we begin to believe that there's a demon behind every situation. That is just not so. It is easy to say, *"The devil Made Me Do It"* instead of owning up to our own lust, anger or other failures.

People have a "Free Will" to make decisions and they often times use poor judgment and make wrong decisions that can affect others. Blaming demons is popular because it hides the evil in our own hearts. "The heart is deceitful above all things, and desperately wicked: who can know it" **Jeremiah 17:9**

Jesus said, "Not that which goes into the mouth defiles a man, but that which cometh out of the mouth, this defiles a man." **Mathew**

15:11 So blaming evil forces for what we do is not religiously correct.

The other error in fighting demonic influences is…not believing that demonic activity is real and that it never affects you. Jesus cast out demons. His disciples did also and for centuries the church has faced demonic activity.

Here's a partial list of situations that might indicate that you are under demonic control or attack.

- Thinking thoughts "that are not yours."

- Having sudden depression.

- Having suicidal thoughts.

- Having fits of anger or rage that are unusual for you.

- Feeling hopeless.

- Your pets start acting differently around you.

- Your close friends start questioning your thinking or behavior.

- Excessive fatigue.

- Not being able to do what you know is good or right.

- Feeling like you are being pulled to do the wrong thing.

- Feeling like you are being pressured to do something you don't want to do.

- Hearing voices or thoughts in your head that are negative, persuasive, or commanding you to do something.

- Deep or severe personality changes like fear or wanting to be isolated all the time.

- Suddenly having creepy or scary feelings.

- Recent feelings that an area, like in your house, there is something heavy, depressive or oppressive.

- Feelings of being under attack or threatened when others don't.

- Finding it hard or impossible to pray.

- Finding it harder or impossible to spend time with Christian brothers or sisters.

- Sudden and unexplainable anxiety.

- Sudden development of Lupus or other auto immune system decease.

Some medical problems can cause similar conditions. It could be from a new bad habit or an encounter with a sinful situation or circumstance. If this is true, you know what to do. Repent and move on with your life. Trust Jesus. (The above list is an excerpt from Pastor Thomas of The Joseph Plan World Wide Ministry) ministry@thejosephplan.org

The best way to dispel demonic activity in your life is to call upon the name of the Lord and command that demon to leave you, *in the name of Jesus*. Then draw close to God, through prayer and seek His Divine revelation as to what to do next.

He will most likely send you to His Word to read and listen as He speaks to you from the pages of the bible. You will get all the direction you need to overcome and demonic influence.

Remember, Resist the devil and he will flee from you. To resist is to quote scripture, as Jesus did in the wilderness.

Why Me Lord

If you are like me, you probably said, *"Why Me Lord."* There was a time when I thought I could be neutral, just doing my own thing but still believing in God. The problem with that sort of thinking is that can not be.

We were created to be the image and likemess of God here on this earth. God went to a lot of trouble to create and enact a plan that would accomplish this. With the fall of Adam and the entire human race, we were left with being the image of Satan. Now our "Free Will" choice is to stay with the deeds of the flesh, which is the nature of evil or to be, "Born Again" and receive the Spirit of God. There is no neutral ground.

There are some believers who falsely believe that if they have a lot of faith they will not undergo any suffering, severe tests or satanic attacks. Nothing could be further from the truth! Actually, the opposite is true.

First Peter 5:8-9 teaches that Satan roams the earth seeking someone to devour. When we read the context, we can come to the conclusion that the devil's main focus is to distract and disarm the children of God. Consequently, when someone on earth wants to bring the influence of the kingdom of God on earth as it is in heaven, Satan fights back to keep the earth under his control.

This is why it seems as though a person following the will of God will sometimes have the most difficult tests, trials and resistance, as opposed to some saints who are casual seekers of God.

Satan is no dummy, why should he attack a Christian who is a bad example to others and who is already deceived and in his grip? He will focus rather on those who are the biggest threat to his authority and rule Remember: God gave Adam a commission to have His rule over the whole earth (Gen. 1:28), and immediately after that the devil came and convinced both Adam and Eve to disobey God and abandon their posts as God's vice regents over the earth **(Gen. 3:1-8).**

Since that time Satan has been jealously attempting to protect his control over the earthly realm which he stole through subverting Adam, including its systems of government, commerce, media, the arts, science and education.

Those who attempt to bring Gods' influence in these areas will most likely experience some of the highest levels of satanic resistance. The apostle Paul had a messenger from Satan follow him everywhere he went that caused riots and persecutions **(2 Cor. 13:1-8),** only because he was turning the present world system upside down **(Acts 17:7).**

So, if you are sold out for God, don't be discouraged when you are attacked or allow yourself to be deceived into thinking that the only reason you are in intense spiritual warfare or tribulation is because you may have missed God. It may be the opposite. You are being targeted because you are hitting the devine bullseye! This is why Paul admonished believers to stand strong in the Lord: "Our struggle is not against flesh and blood but against principalities, powers and the rulers of darkness in high places" **(Ephesians 6:10-13)**.

Notice: Paul said "our struggle" meaning he was including himself in this struggle. Every time there was an open door for ministry he had many adversaries. This is a biblical principle **(read 1 Corinthians 16:9).**

Do not ever think that just because God is calling you to do something that it will be easy. Jesus did the will of God and He was crucified, and church history tells us Paul was beheaded! It's not how many years we live, but what we do with the years we live that matters!

So, what do we do when we are in a time of spiritual warfare that Paul calls "the day of evil" in Ephesians 6:13? Paul tells us in this passage to be strong in the Lord and to stand firm; in other words, do not quit (Eph. 6:10-13).

The apostle Peter also tells us to resist the devil, standing firm in the faith (1 Pet. 5:9). Peter knew firsthand that faith in God is the key to standing firm in the midst of the day of evil because, when he denied Christ three times, Jesus prayed for him that his "faith" would not fail (Luke 22:31-32).

So, do not be afraid when you are in tribulation, because Jesus has already overcome the world (John 16:33)!

We are privilaged to stand up for our faith and belief in Jesus Christ. We should take every oportunity to share our faith and stand for what is right, no matter what others think.

What To Do Next

The Bible gives us clear instruction on how to keep ourselves free, healthy and happy in a world that is a battleground where Satan seeks to kill, steal and destroy. (John 10:10) Here's a recap of what we can do next to keep our hearts:

Be transformed-…Romans 12:2; Cast down imaginations-…2 Corinthians 10:5; Bring into captivity every thought to the obedience of Christ; 2 Corinthians 10:5; Be spiritually minded-Romans 8:6; Put off the old man-Ephesians 4:22; Be renewed in your mind-Ephesians 4:23; Put on the new man-Ephesians 4:24; Let the mind of Christ be in you- Philippians 5; Let no man beguile you-Colossians 2:18; Let no man spoil you-Colossians 2:8; Be fully persuaded in your mind-Romans 14:5; Do not have a doubtful mind-Luke 12:29; Do not be soon shaken in mind-2 Thessalonians 2:2; Do not Be troubled-2 Thessalonians 2:2; Gird up the loins of your mind-1 Peter 1:13; Be sober-1 Peter 1:13 and above all Hope to the end for the grace of God-1 Peter.

I am sure you will find more things as you read the scripture but these will make a great starting place. Just remember, God is always with you. He is not mad at you, nor does He expect you to win every time. Your salvation does not hang in the balance. If you fail, He will just pick you up and help you along the way until you can sit, walk and stand in faith.

Signs of The End of The Age And The Rise of Satanic Influences

We have all been told that the end of the world is at hand. Hollywood has even made movies on how it might happen. I want to show some of the rise of Satanic influences and how it will affect us. Let's first look at what Jesus said about the end times as recorded in Matthew 24.

"See that no one leads you astray. [5] *For* [b]*many will come in my name, saying, 'I am* [c]*the Christ,' and they will lead many astray.* [6] And you will hear of wars and rumors of wars. See that you are not alarmed, for this must take place, but the end is not yet. [7] For nation will rise against nation, and kingdom against kingdom, and there will be famines and earthquakes in various places. [8] All these are but the beginning of the birth pains." Matthew 24:4-8

"And many [o]false prophets will arise [p]and lead many astray. [12] And because lawlessness will be increased, the love of many will grow cold: Matthew 24: 11-12. "For false christs and false prophets will arise and perform great signs and wonders, so as to lead astray, if possible, even the elect." **Matthew 24:24**

"Let no man deceive you by any means: for that day shall not come, *except there come a falling away first*, and that man of sin be revealed, the son of perdition;: **II Thessalonians 2:3**

Here's what I see in these scriptures

1. Many will come in His Name saying they are Christ. This, in my opinion, refers to false Christians. They say they are of the Christian Faith but do not follow the doctrine that the Apostles taught. The Mormons call themselves Latter Day Saints and have changed the gospel to fit their own perspectives. They are deceiving many and taking them away from the true Gospel.

2. Other groups, known as the Occults do the same thing.

3. Modern day churches, both Protestant and Catholic are full of folks that example doctrine of devils, yet they claim to be Christians.

It is obvious that false prophets have come onto the world stage, as though they were a "Pied Piper", and they have led many astray. It is also obvious that there has been, over the last 50 years, a great falling away from the faith and doctrines taught by Jesus and His apostles.

I said all of that to say this. The same demons that led many to follow false prophets to believe in doctrines of devils in the 1st century are still here, hard at work, to take us down. We need to recognize what is happening around us. We need to discern the times we live in and we need to discover and apply the weapons of our warfare so we do not get lost in the crowd that is being led astray.

The battle of the ages is for the souls of mankind. It all takes place in the minds of every human being. Before wars break out between countries, battles are fought and lost in the minds of the leaders of those nations. To survive in a life and death struggle for our soul, we will absolutely need to be able to recognize our enemy, know his dirty tricks and schemes, and what weapons God has provided for us to defend ourselves and even win the battle.

We will need to realize that Jesus has defeated every evil force and given us power over them. We need to know that this battle of the ages is the Lords. He knows exactly what to do, when to do it and who to send into the battle to take back what the devil has stolen.

We need to realize that God rested on the seventh day of creation from *all* His works. That means He knew all about us, our temptations, concerns, needs and how to cause us to attain victory.

In other words, He has a master plan that is being worked out in the earth. All we need to do is trust Him, believe His Word, apply His counsel and rest in His finished work of Grace.

PART II ...THE BELIEVER'S AUTHORITY

Part II will call attention to the authority that a believer. We will be looking at Bible verses that document real authority given to followers of Christ. Authority that was given by Jesus to the 1st century followers and is still available today.

We will look at some myths, some logic and some Biblical examples to gain a full picture. We will discuss the now and how and when this authority operates.

The biggest and most powerful lie that Satan uses to defeat the church of Jesus Christ is, "You do not have the authority to take charge and rule over evil forces." The devil keeps telling us that but guess what? When Jesus ascended, after his resurrection, He left us power.

The lie that has persisted in Christian circles and has become a dogma is... that all that miracle working power ended with the death of the Apostles. This heresy is now commonplace and believed by most evangelicals.

Do you have power from on high to overcome evil by casting out demons, healing the sick, binding Satan from your thoughts or changing the outcome of a circumstance? Most folks are afraid to even try. They shy away from seeking the Lord for a Word of

Wisdom or a Word of Knowledge that would help them to better know and accomplish God's Will.

Do you read the Bible, as it were, a history book? Or is it alive with revelation and truth that stirs up your faith and builds your confidence to act upon what is being communicated to you by the Holy Spirit?

What if I told you that you have authority as a believer? The same authority that Jesus had and still has is yours. All you need is to engage your believer and receive it.

You can become the head and not the tail. "And the LORD shall make thee the head, and not the tail; and thou shalt be above only, and thou shalt not be beneath; if that thou hearken unto the commandments of the LORD thy God, which I command thee this day, to observe and to do *them*:" **Deut. 28:13**

You can live a victorious life. You just need to believe. How do I know, because Jesus said so? "The thief cometh not, but for to steal, and to kill, and to destroy: I am come that they might have life, and that they might have *it* more abundantly." **John 10:10**

The Source of Your Authority

We can all agree, I think, that the source of our Spiritual authority comes from Jesus. It was He that spoiled the principalities and powers of evil. "*And* having spoiled principalities and powers, he made a shew of them openly, triumphing over them in it." **Colossians 2:15** It was He that died for our sins as a penalty. "For he hath made him *to be* sin for us, who knew no sin; that we might be made the righteousness of God in him." **II Cor. 5:21**

It was Jesus that gave His followers authority over unclean spirits and sent them out two by two. "And he called *unto him* the twelve, and began to send them forth by two and two; and gave them power over unclean spirits;" **Mark 6:7**

It was Jesus that said, "And I will pray the Father, and he shall give you another Comforter, that he may abide with you for ever." **John 14:16** This other comforter is none other than the Holy Spirit that baptized the 120 in the upper room on the day of Pentecost.

Now Hear This...

When the Spirit came on the day of Pentecost, He filled everyone with His presence and power. They spoke in other tongues and eventually went out from the upper room to preach, teach, do miracles and walk in the Spirit. Jesus did not abandon them. He sent His Holy Spirit to deliver His power and authority to His church and to become the source of continued power to live in Christ.

Listen to what Paul said to Timothy. "For God has not given us a spirit of fear, but of power and of love and of a sound mind. **II Timothy 1:7** "This *is* the word of the Lord to Zerubbabel: 'Not by might nor by power, but by My Spirit,' Says the Lord of hosts. **Zechariah 4:6** Thus, our authority is given by God, through Jesus and made accessible through the Holy Spirit.

My Dad was a police officer. He was endowed with the power and authority of the government. He knew he had authority and so did the crooks that ran from him when he showed up at the location of a crime

We who believe understand that in the name of Jesus we have

an even mightier authority than that what the government gave my dad. In **Matthew 28:18**, Jesus said, *...all power [authority] is given unto me in heaven and in earth.*

Jesus has given this authority to His followers.

Luke 9:1, 2 says, *Then he called his twelve disciples together, and gave them power and **authority** over all devils, and to cure diseases. And he sent them to preach the kingdom of God, and to heal the sick.*

Mark 13:34 tells us, *for the Son of man is as a man taking a far journey, who left his house, and gave authority to his servants, and to every man his work, and commanded the porter to watch.*

And he said unto them, Go ye into all the world, and preach the gospel to every creature. ... And these signs shall follow them that believe; In my name shall they cast out devils; they shall speak with new tongues; they shall take up serpents; and if they drink any deadly thing, it shall not hurt them; they shall lay hands on the sick, and they shall recover. **Mark 16:15, 17, 18**.

Clearly, Jesus has promised His authority to those who are His own. The problem is that "His Own" do not believe it, and therefore do not exercise it.

Many Christians refuse to believe that Christ's authority belongs to the Church today -- although there is no Scripture that in any way hints that His authority would *not* be available to the Church through all the ages. Many are content just reading about the miracles that took place. Some of us may go so far as to dare to command a sickness or a devil to be gone from someone we are praying for, but we are fairly complacent when nothing happens. It is what we were expecting anyway, isn't it? What we are forgetting is that the devil is not a law-abiding citizen. *He is the lawless one.*

What happens when the police officer attempts to use his authority, and finds himself resisted? Does he shrug his shoulders and say, "Well, I guess that didn't work!" No, he pursues and subdues the law-breaker. Sometimes there is a fight -- but the lawful authority wins in the end!

So it is with our authority as believers. We need to understand that the infinitely powerful government of heaven backs us up. Jesus Himself is the one who has given us authority. It is in His Name. Most of the time there *is* a fight. Hell doesn't want to let go of its victims. We need to pursue, press in, and insist on being obeyed. *And from the days of John the Baptist until now the kingdom of heaven suffers violence, and the violent take it by force.* -- **Matthew 11:12**. Sometimes the police officer needs to use force. Sometimes the believer does, too.

There are some qualifications, which we must meet in order to have rightful authority in Christ. Let's continue to look at parallels between the police officer and the Christian.

1. The police officer must be under authority himself, obedient to his superiors. He goes where he has been assigned, not outside his jurisdiction. We must be doing what Jesus has said, according to the Bible and His personal word to us as well. We cannot be out doing our own thing for our own pleasure. *A clean, submitted heart is imperative.*

2. The police officer must continue to stay in contact with his superiors, and must get their direction as needed in difficult situations. We need to be in constant communication with Jesus.

3. The police officer must know how to use his weapons, or his opponent will run roughshod over him, and maybe kill him. We must be skillful in the use of our weapons -- the Blood of Jesus, the Name of Jesus, our faith. Especially, we have to know the Word of God and use it properly.

4. The police officer must understand the law and not step outside its boundaries. He can't arrest people if they haven't broken the law. We must understand what Jesus has given us and what He has not. If it's in the Book it's ours to use. If it's not clearly in the Book, we're on shaky ground. We need to research from Genesis to Revelation to make sure we're getting it right. *Know the Word.*

Remember whose authority it is in which we operate. We have no authority to come against the powers of darkness in our own strength. We come against them in the *Name of Jesus.* It is His authority, not ours.

Attempting to execute authority for anything other than His plans, His will, His desires is presumption. It will most certainly fail --and may put us in grave danger as well.

If something is important to you, you will go after it. The things God has promised us in His Word should be vitally important to us -- enough so that we are prepared to take hold and struggle for them at any cost until we obtain them. Anything worth having is worth fighting for. (Article prepared by **Lee Ann Rubsam**)

A Kenneth E. Hagin Perspective About The Authority of The Believer

I get upset when I hear people being afraid or in fear of the devil. "You'd better be careful! The devil might hear you."

I practice what Kenneth Hagin teaches. He said, "I have authority over myself and my house. If the devil ever comes knocking at my door with sickness, poverty, lack, or oppression, I tell him, don't come to my house. You'll have to go peddle that junk somewhere else because I won't receive it!"

But I don't have authority over the devil in your life. Ultimately you'll have to learn to stand against the devil for yourself. God will expect you to take authority over the devil for yourself.

Take authority over the powers of darkness, sickness, disease, or whatever the enemy brings your way. Stand against it for yourself in the Name of Jesus.

Failing to recognize that the Greater One dwells in you will cause you to fall when attacked. You will be defeated if you don't recognize the authority you have in Christ. It's one thing for Satan to dominate unsaved people who are in the kingdom of darkness; they're under his authority. We don't want to be numbered among them.

Too often Christians just hang on and try to do the best they can, not realizing what their inheritance in Christ really entitles them to. Instead of taking their rightful place in Christ as victors, they complain and fear the devil, which gives him access in their lives.

I know Jesus defeated the devil, that's what I think on and talk about. And the Greater One, (Holy Spirit), puts me over in life and causes me to succeed because I'm giving place to God and the power of His Word, not to the devil. http://www.cfaith.com

Exposing The Enemy

Whether you realize it or not, Satan knows your strengths and weaknesses. He is watching for opportunities to catch you off guard so he can slip in and cause trouble. When that happens, he hopes you will be like many other Christians and put the blame elsewhere. He loves to hear, "If it wasn't for my parents or losing my job, or whatever, I'd be somebody."

As a subtle manipulator of circumstances, the devil tries to hide his activities by making you blame events, people, or even God for the destructive things he does. Make no mistake about it: your parents, your spouse, your children, your pastor, your employer, God – none of these are the real enemy.

Who is the enemy? Ephesians 6:12 says, *"We do not wrestle against flesh and blood, but against principalities, against powers, against the rulers of the darkness of this age, against spiritual hosts of wickedness in the heavenly places."* The devil is the real enemy!

Like A Roaring Lion

1 Peter 5:8-9 (NIV) advises us to: *"Be self-controlled and alert. Your enemy the devil prowls around like a roaring lion looking for someone to devour. Resist him, standing firm in the faith..."* Notice that this verse does not say the devil is a roaring lion. It

says he is like a roaring lion. He wants to make you believe he has more power than he really does, and he manages to fool the majority of people. The truth is, the devil's only weapon is that of deception. He has no legal authority over believers.

When Jesus died and rose again, He not only saved you from an eternity in hell, He also redeemed you from Satan's power and dominion. **1 John 3:8** tells us, *"For this purpose the Son of God was manifested, that He might destroy the works of the devil."*

Not only that, but it is recorded in Colossians 2:15 that Jesus *"disarmed principalities and powers,"* and *"He made a public spectacle of them, triumphing over them..."* The devil is already defeated, and his power has been destroyed by the finished work of Christ on the cross.

You Have Authority

Jesus said, *"Behold, I give you the authority to trample on serpents and scorpions, and over all the power of the enemy, and nothing shall by any means hurt you"* (Luke 10:19). That is a great deal of authority!

Why then, does the devil cause believers so much trouble? It is because many do not exercise the authority God has given them. They are not walking in the understanding that they need to enforce that victory Jesus attained on the cross in their daily lives.

Think of it this way: it is illegal for someone to break into your house, but don't you still lock your doors to discourage thieves and to protect your property? In the same way, when it comes to Satan trying to gain entrance into your life, you need to exercise your blood-bought right to close the door in his face. By resisting the devil and standing firm in the faith, you are actively enforcing Jesus' victory.

God has given you all the authority you need to be able to stand against the devil. He has also provided you with armor and spiritual weapons. In his letter to the Ephesians, the apostle Paul describes these items and defines how to use them. He writes, *"Be strong in the Lord and in the power of His might. Put on the whole armor of God that you may be able to stand against the wiles of the devil. Take up the whole armor of God, that you may be able to withstand in the evil day, and having done all, to stand"* **(Ephesians 6:10-11, 13).**

Paul made it clear that, while God has provided the armor, it is the believer's responsibility to put it on and stand against the enemy. We must take our position of authority and use what God has given us.

In The Name of Jesus

The name of Jesus is powerful. Philippians 2:9-10 says, *"Therefore God also has highly exalted Him and given Him the name which is above every name, that at the name of Jesus every knee should bow, of those in heaven, and of those on earth, and of those under the earth..."* When you use Jesus' name, Satan's strongholds cannot stand **(see 2 Corinthians 10:4).**

Think of using the name of Jesus the same way you would use a key to unlock a door. It doesn't matter if the key belongs to you or not, if you have it in your hand you can use it to open the door. It is the same with the name of Jesus. Jesus won the victory. Power over the devil is rightfully His, but He has given you the authority to use His name. You have His authority in your hand.

Try using Jesus' name today to take authority over the devil and his works in the name of Jesus. When you command him to leave, he must obey just as if Jesus were commanding him **(see Mark 16:17)**. You can say, "Sickness, go in the name of Jesus" or "Depression, you must leave in Jesus' name" or "devil, in the name of Jesus, get out of here!" He has to leave because of the authority that is in Jesus' name.

Keep The Devil Out

Ephesians 4:27 tells us not to give any place to the devil. Whether you have been a believer for a day or twenty years, keep building your relationship with God through daily Bible reading, meditating on the Word, and prayer. Be part a good Bible-believing church, and start worshiping God. When it comes to keeping the devil out, there is no substitute for godly living.

If you are not careful you can give the devil power by entertaining sin, being disobedient, or by rebelling against God. Make sure you are quick to forgive others as Christ has forgiven you because having an unwillingness to forgive others can give the devil a foothold in your life **(Mark 11:25).**

James 4:7 instructs us to, *"Submit to God. Resist the devil and he will flee from you."* Because Jesus resisted the devil by submitting to God, He could say, *"...he (the devil) has nothing in Me"* **(John 14:30)**. He left no room for the devil to take advantage of Him. Likewise, when you submit to God and resist the devil in the authority Christ has given you, the devil must leave.

Finally...

The victory Christ won, He won for you. After He rose from the grave, victorious over death, sin, and the grave, He proclaimed, *"All authority has been given to Me in heaven and on earth"* **(Matthew 28:18)**. When you received Christ as the Lord of your life, **Colossians 1:13** says you were delivered from the power of darkness and conveyed into the God's kingdom.

You can take a bold stand against the devil and his works because of your position in Christ and because you have been given authority over Satan in the name of Jesus. As **Proverbs 28:1** says, *"The wicked flee when no one pursues, but the righteous are bold as a lion."*

Submit to God, boldly exercise the authority He has given you, and stand firm because, *"He who is in you is greater than he who is in the world"* **(1 John 4:4)**.

Five Reasons Believers Don't Walk In The Power And Authority They Have In Christ.
(Presented by Charisma Magazine)

1. Sin.... When we habitually sin, we come under Satan's authority, and he has legal rights over us until we repent. That is why Jesus said, "'The ruler of this world is coming, and has nothing on Me'" (John 14:30, NKJV). Jesus was without sin, so the devil could not get a foothold in His life.

James 5:16 declares, "The effective, fervent prayer of a righteous man avails much." This verse points out that authority is given to the righteous. Carlos Annacondia, an Argentine evangelist, once told me that he believes God gave him more authority when he became ruthless about his sin and the sin in his family's life.

Along the same line, we have to be under authority before we can exercise authority. If we are rebellious toward our parents or the authority of our church, we won't have much authority over the evil one.

2. Ignorance.... In Hosea 4:6, God declares, "'My people are destroyed for lack of knowledge.'" The Lord showed me that His people are being destroyed by the ignorance of their authority in Christ. Yet the Bible makes it clear that we are not powerless against the enemy.

Second Corinthians 10:3-5 states, "For though we walk in the flesh, we do not war according to the flesh. For the weapons of our warfare are not carnal but mighty in God for pulling down strongholds, casting down arguments and every high thing that exalts itself against the knowledge of God, bringing every thought into captivity to the obedience of Christ."

Many believers tend to see the cosmic struggle through the lens of the Asian philosophy of yin and yang, which contends that good and evil forces are opposite each other but equal in power and authority. In reality, Satan is a loser. He is a created being, one of God's fallen angels.

God, on the other hand, is the uncreated Creator who always has been and always will be--He is self-existent. To a believer who is walking in God's authority, Satan is like a toothless lion. It is not that Satan doesn't have some real power--he does. But when we compare his power with God's--there is no comparison.

When David confronted Goliath, Goliath compared his physical prowess with David's. Goliath was insulted that the Israelites would send a mere shepherd boy against him.

However, David didn't compare himself with Goliath; he compared Goliath with God. God was so much greater than Goliath that the match was over before it had a chance to begin (see 1 Sam. 17:41-50).

In observing God's people, I have noticed that way too many of us tend to be ignorant about the source of evil. Satan, not God, is the cause of all the evil in the world. When we have a warped perspective of the sovereignty of God, we become passive in fighting sickness and evil.

After the historic 9/11 tragedy, I was amazed to discover how many people attributed the terrorist attacks to God's judgment. The Bible tells us that Satan--not God--is the one who comes to kill, steal and destroy (see John 10:10) and that we are to put on the full armor of God and stand firm against the evil one (see Eph. 6:10-18).

3. Unbelief.... Unbelief is a serious sin. Romans 14:23 reads, "But the man who has doubts is condemned if he eats, because his eating is not from faith; and everything that does not come from faith is sin." The book of Hebrews also calls unbelief sinful: "See to it, brothers, that none of you has a sinful, unbelieving heart that turns away from the living God" (3:12). Unbelief is so serious that Jesus could not do many miracles because of the people's lack of faith (see Matt. 13:58).

We can measure the level of our belief or unbelief by asking ourselves, Do we really believe that Jesus defeated the enemy? If we don't, we are unlikely to see the results we desire when we lay hands on the sick.

4. Fear.... Second Timothy 1:7-8 declares, "God has not given us a spirit of fear." Fear paralyzes us and keeps us from wielding the authority we have in Christ to bring healing to others.

First **John 5:18** teaches us that "the wicked one does not touch [whoever is born of God]" **(see also Luke 10:19)**. But some people have suffered backlash from the enemy when they engaged in spiritual warfare and are now afraid.

There are many reasons for backlash. Here are some ways to guard against it: Be led by the Spirit; make sure that Satan has no legal right to attack; and obtain prayer covering.

After taking these steps, we can confront the darkness because we have the authority to do so. We need not be afraid of obeying God's directives even if it requires engaging in strategic warfare.

Luke 12:32 gives us wise counsel: "'Do not be afraid, little flock, for it is your Father's good pleasure to give you the kingdom.'"

5. Lack of Prayer.... Luke 18:1 establishes the importance of prayer: "Then Jesus told His disciples a parable to show them that they should always pray and not give up" (NIV).

Ephesians 6:18 elaborates on this point: "And pray in the Spirit on all occasions with all kinds of prayers and requests. With this in mind, be alert and always keep on praying for all the saints."

Evangelist Winkie Pratney once told a story about a pastor's wife who was jogging one day when she saw a man dressed in white standing in a cornfield. The pastor's wife had been going through a difficult trial, and when she saw this man, whom she recognized as Jesus, He said to her: "Don't you know who I am? Don't you know who you are? When you know this, it is not really as hard as you think."

There is a lesson here for all of us. When we know who God is and the authority He has, and when we know who we are in Christ, having faith is not that difficult. And when we have faith, we will begin to release the spiritual authority necessary to perform signs, wonders and miracles.

(Article written by Ché Ahn is senior pastor of Harvest Rock Church in Pasadena, California, and founder and president of Harvest International Ministries, a worldwide network of approximately 1,000 churches and ministries.)

The Now, The How And The When
This Authority Operates

Today's Christian's want instant results. I prayed for healing so why didn't it happen? It's been 10 minutes already with no change. I thought it would be NOW not later or not at all. HOW does this authority/ Power, work? WHEN will I see results?

Sometimes there is a pathway on which we must walk to our healing or to see results. Sometimes we see it immediately. The final result is up to God. We are to pray, believe and proclaim in the name of Jesus. He will make it happen as He sees fit.

I can remember a time we prayed for a lady to be healed. It actually took seven months of continual prayer and continual proclaiming of God's Word. My wife prayed for a lady's leg and vein problems. She was healed in that very hour.

The point is, don't give up because you do not see any change. You declare the Word, Believe the Word and Stand in faith until what you have declared comes into existence. (For we walk by faith, not by sight:) **II Cor. 5:7**

Remember, it is the Word that carries all the power and it is your faith and trust in Jesus that what He said is true that gives you the authority.

Some Myths And Some Logic

1. **Myth**…We don't have to do anything because Jesus did it all. **Logic…** If that were true, Jesus would not have commanded us to go into the World and preach the gospel. He would have done it Himself.

   We are privileged to participate and see God's power transferred from God to Jesus to His Holy Spirit to us. What a joy to actually see Satan run away at the mention of Jesus and his evil works spoiled at the speaking of the Word of God. We are the head, not the tail. The devil is defeated.

2. **Myth**…There is no evil force that sways our thinking. It is all our decisions. **Logic**…Yes we do make bad decisions and some even sinful or in rebellion to God. But, the apostles told us that we have an enemy that is out to get us. Who do we believe, those that were taught by Jesus or those who deny God and mock our faith?

3. **Myth**…The Bible is just a book and has no final authority over anything. **Logic…** The Bible is actually 66 books. It took thousands of years to come into being and translated into multiple languages. It is full of history, faith, and promises from God, counsel, and a lot more. It is the source of Faith to the believer and

a Lifeline to divine revelation. It has outlasted wars, heretics, atheists, and all the rest of Satan's attacks. One only has to read it to discover that it is indeed the Word of God.

4. **Myth**…The believer's authority was given only to His immediate followers. When they died, the gifts stopped. **Logic**…It was the gifts that proved that Jesus was who He said He was. It was the passing on of the gifts by the laying on of hands that became a blessing to future believers. The world has 20+ times the population as was in Jesus' day. Doesn't it seem logical that the gifts would be even more in demand and needed in our day? To end them abruptly is to leave us comfortless and Jesus said He would not do that.

Two Biblical Examples of The Believer's Authority

Ephesians 6:10-18 …"Finally, be strong in the Lord and in the strength of his might. Put on the whole armor of God, that you may be able to stand against the schemes of the devil. For we do not wrestle against flesh and blood, but against the rulers, against the authorities, against the cosmic powers over this present darkness, against the spiritual forces of evil in the heavenly places. Therefore take up the whole armor of God, that you may be able to withstand in the evil day, and having done all, to stand firm. Stand therefore, having fastened on the belt of truth, and having put on the breastplate of righteousness," … **God has given us His armor but we must put it on and use it.**

Matthew 14:25-29…"And in the fourth watch of the night Jesus went unto them, walking on the sea. [26] And when the disciples saw him walking on the sea, they were troubled, saying, It is a spirit; and they cried out for fear. [27] But straightway Jesus spake unto them, saying, Be of good cheer; it is I; be not afraid. [28] And Peter answered him and said, Lord, if it be thou, bid me come unto thee on the water. [29] And he said, Come. And when Peter was come down out of the ship, he walked on the water, to go to Jesus"…..**Jesus has the authority or power to walk on water. Peter did not until Jesus bid him to come**. Then he stepped out by faith, trusting in that power or authority and walked on the water… until he took his eyes off of Jesus and looked at the raging sea. He still had the power but decided, because of the fear, to cry out for help. It's called, "Faith Failure". We have them all the time.

Bible References Related To The Believer's Authority

Mark 16:17 …And these signs will accompany those who believe: in my name they will cast out demons; they will speak in new tongues;

James 4:7 …Submit yourselves therefore to God. Resist the devil, and he will flee from you.

Luke 10:19 …Behold, I have given you authority to tread on serpents and scorpions, and over all the power of the enemy, and nothing shall hurt you.

Matthew 16:19 …I will give you the keys of the kingdom of heaven, and whatever you bind on earth shall be bound in heaven, and whatever you loose on earth shall be loosed in heaven."

1 Peter 5:8 …Be sober-minded; be watchful. Your adversary the devil prowls around like a roaring lion, seeking someone to devour.

Luke 10:19-21 …Behold, I have given you authority to tread on serpents and scorpions, and over all the power of the enemy, and nothing shall hurt you. Nevertheless, do not rejoice in this, that the spirits are subject to you, but rejoice that your names are written in heaven. In that same hour he rejoiced in the Holy Spirit and said, "I thank you, Father, Lord of heaven and earth, that you have hidden these things from the wise and understanding and revealed them to little children; yes, Father, for such was your gracious will."

1 John 4:4 … Little children, you are from God and have overcome them, for he who is in you is greater than he who is in the world.

Revelation 12:11 …And they have conquered him by the blood of the Lamb and by the word of their testimony, for they loved not their lives even unto death.

Mark 11:23 …Truly, I say to you, whoever says to this mountain, 'Be taken up and thrown into the sea,' and does not doubt in his heart, but believes that what he says will come to pass, it will be done for him.

Hebrews 4:12 …For the word of God is living and active, sharper than any two-edged sword, piercing to the division of soul and of spirit, of joints and of marrow, and discerning the thoughts and intentions of the heart.

Acts 1:8 …But you will receive power when the Holy Spirit has come upon you, "and you will be my witnesses in Jerusalem and in all Judea and Samaria, and to the end of the earth."

John 14:12 …"Truly, truly, I say to you, whoever believes in me will also do the works that I do; and greater works than these will he do, because I am going to the Father."

Luke 10:17-19 …The seventy-two returned with joy, saying, "Lord, even the demons are subject to us in your name!" And he said to them, "I saw Satan fall like lightning from heaven. Behold, I have given you authority to tread on serpents and scorpions, and over all the power of the enemy, and nothing shall hurt you."

Mark 6:13 …And they cast out many demons and anointed with oil many who were sick and healed them.

Ephesians 6:10-18 …Finally, be strong in the Lord and in the strength of his might. Put on the whole armor of God, that you may be able to stand against the schemes of the devil. For we do not wrestle against flesh and blood, but against the rulers, against the authorities, against the cosmic powers over this present darkness, against the spiritual forces of evil in the heavenly places. Therefore take up the whole armor of God, that you may be able to withstand in the evil day, and having done all, to stand firm. Stand therefore, having fastened on the belt of truth, and having put on the breastplate of righteousness, …

Matthew 28:18-20 …And Jesus came and said to them, "All authority in heaven and on earth has been given to me. Go therefore and make disciples of all nations, baptizing them in the name of the Father and of the Son and of the Holy Spirit, teaching them to observe all that I have commanded you. And behold, I am with you always, to the end of the age."

Psalm 91:13 ...You will tread on the lion and the adder; the young lion and the serpent you will trample underfoot.

Acts 2:39 ...For the promise is for you and for your children and for all who are far off, everyone whom the Lord our God calls to himself.

Matthew 10:1 ...And he called to him his twelve disciples and gave them authority over unclean spirits, to cast them out, and to heal every disease and every affliction.

Acts 16:18 ...And this she kept doing for many days. Paul, having become greatly annoyed, turned and said to the spirit, "I command you in the name of Jesus Christ to come out of her." And it came out that very hour.

Acts 3:6 ...But Peter said, "I have no silver and gold, but what I do have I give to you. In the name of Jesus Christ of Nazareth, rise up and walk!"

Luke 10:1-42 ...After this the Lord appointed seventy-two others and sent them on ahead of him, two by two, into every town and place where he himself was about to go. And he said to them, "The harvest is plentiful, but the laborers are few. Therefore pray earnestly to the Lord of the harvest to send out laborers into his harvest. Go your way; behold, I am sending you out as lambs in the midst of wolves. Carry no moneybag, no knapsack, no sandals, and greet no one on the road. Whatever house you enter, first say, 'Peace be to this house!' ...

Acts 2:1-47 ...When the day of Pentecost arrived; they were all together in one place. And suddenly there came from heaven a sound like a mighty rushing wind, and it filled the entire house where they were sitting. And divided tongues as of fire appeared to them and rested on each one of them. And they were all filled with the Holy Spirit and began to speak in other tongues as the Spirit gave them utterance. Now there were dwelling in Jerusalem Jews, devout men from every nation under heaven. ...

Revelation 12:10 ... And I heard a loud voice in heaven, saying, "Now the salvation and the power and the kingdom of our God and the authority of his Christ have come, for the accuser of our brothers has been thrown down, who accuses them day and night before our God."

1 Corinthians 12:8 ... For to one is given through the Spirit the utterance of wisdom, and to another the utterance of knowledge according to the same Spirit,

We have the Spiritual authority or power of Jesus at our disposal. We can use it or not. If we don't, we will remain defeated and live in a carnal world being plagued by evil forces at every turn. It's far more to our advantage to stand up in the Lord and the power of His might and declare our freedom and walk in His Will.

As in most promises of God, it's up to us. God will not invade our free will. He will sit quietly by and watch us fall and then pick us up and start again to teach our hands to war so we can be victorious.

I Am A Believer & I Have Authority To Spoil The Works of The Devil

When you believe, you rely upon, you adhere to and you trust in. That, my friends, is believing with the heart.

PART III...BATTLE STRATEGIES

We will look at 20 scripture passages that can be applied to spiritual warfare. There are multiple strategies that are seldom used to battle Satan but are extremely powerful. I will leave the final judgment up to you as to the correct interpretation of scripture and application. We will let the Bible speak for itself.

The Bible says, "Thy word have I hid in mine heart, that I might not sin against thee." **Psalm 119:11** It also says, "For the word of God is quick, and powerful, and sharper than any two-edged sword, piercing even to the dividing asunder of soul and spirit, and of the joints and marrow, and is a discerner of the thoughts and intents of the heart." **Hebrews 4:12**

If you have not hidden God's Word in your heart, you will not have it at hand to overcome temptation, the flesh, or the oppression of the devil. We must have it at hand and be able to recall it in any situation. We must be ready to speak it out against the attack. We must also rest in the Lord and His Word, knowing that it is able to cut through every difficulty, every attack, bringing clarity to our minds and peace to our souls.

The following are Battle Strategies, weapons of our warfare that are not usually found in the average arsenal.

Being Ready

1. I Peter 5:8 "Be sober, be vigilant; because your adversary the devil, as a roaring lion, walketh about, seeking whom he may devour:"

The first and most important strategy is to be ready at all times. Be sober and vigilant is to expect the attack and any time and be ready to fight back. The battle is in your mind. That is where it all takes place.

We are victorious or defeated by how we look at life and what we think. If we allow negative thoughts into our thinking, we will no doubt become negative and fall into depression, a low self-esteem and sadness. Our emotional state will be less than happy and well adjusted.

We must, above all else, know that there is a real enemy that roams this earth seeking a prey that is unaware so he can devour it. Jesus made this clear when He said, "The thief comes not but to steal, kill and destroy" **John 10:10b**

Satan will often use those that are the closes to us to cast his fiery dart into our soul. The people are unaware but nevertheless become instruments in the hands of an angry evil being that is bent on our destruction. He will seek to steal your joy, kill your dreams, and destroy your destiny.

I am sure you have heard the zing of a fiery dart before. It goes like this, "You will never amount to anything." "It's ok to participate in sex before marriage." "It's the norm of a new minimum." "There is no God. We came from apes" and so on. Our teachers in school, the media, and even our scientific community live in a world void of God's love and grace because they have believed

Satan's lies. The lies of pro-choice and gay rights are now the accepted norm of our society.

However, this upside down world does not have to be your world. God wants you to know the truth so you can be free from Satan's lies. He wants you to be ready for the attack and well equiped with spiritual ammo to not only quench the fire of his dart but also to defeat his every move. He wants you to have dominion and rule over evil, putting every demon and every evil attack under your feet.

Strategy In Action… be always aware that evil will seek you out and attempt to steal your joy, kill your dreams and destroy your future. Resist him steadfastly in the faith and give him no place in your life.

Fight The Good Fight of Faith

2. James 4:7, "Submit yourselves therefore to God. Resist the devil, and he will flee from you."

Here is a promise that is sure to deliver your soul from the attacks of the devil. This simple tactic will win the day every time. We first submit our will to God and align our thinking to what He wants for us, not what we may think is best. We find His will by reading the scriptures. Once submitted, we are free from ego, self-will and soul-ish ambition. We want what God wants for us. This makes it easy to resist.

The devil usually temps us with evil that is already in our hearts. He wants us to act out what lurks within. Jesus said, "It is not what enters into the mouth that defiles the man, but what proceeds out of the mouth, this defiles the man." **Matthew 15:11**

We all walk around in sin and have a very big appetite for doing things that are not right in the site of God.

If you disagree, listen to what the bible says and be instructed by these passages:

- *"This I say then, Walk in the Spirit, and ye shall not fulfill the lust of the flesh."* **Galatians 5:16**

- *"For the flesh lusts against the Spirit, and the Spirit against the flesh: and these are contrary the one to the other: so that ye cannot do the things that ye would."* **Galatians 5:17**

- *"For what I am doing, I do not understand; for I am not practicing what I would like to do, but I am doing the very thing I hate."* **Romans 7:15 NASV**

- *O foolish Galatians, who hath bewitched you, that ye should not obey the truth, before whose eyes Jesus Christ hath been evidently set forth, crucified among you? This only would I learn of you, Received ye the Spirit by the works of the law, or by the hearing of faith? Are ye so foolish? Having begun in the Spirit, are ye now made perfect by the flesh?* **Galatians 3:1-3**

Resisting the devil is also resisting our base emotions that trip us up and keep us from pleasing God. Once we have denied our flesh the right to rule our thoughts, and placed Christ on the throne of our lives, we can resist the devil, knowing that he has no where to hide in us and no place in our thoughts. It is then, for the moment, until another attack comes, that we overcome and see him flee from us.

This process of submitting and resisting is not really all that hard.

If you are truly following God, you do that normally as a way of life. It becomes second nature. However it is a great strategy because, as the scripture says, "Neither give place to the devil." **Ephesians 4:27** We are admonished to give no place to our enemy.

Once you are aware of the battle, ready and willing to fight, the next step is to equip yourself with the weapons of your warfare. Being equipped is to know how you will be attacked and establishing a good defense. The wilds or tricks of the devil are numerous and can catch or snare an unsuspecting soul.... Ephesians tells us what our primary weapons are. I've stated them before, but it's worth mentioning again.

"Wherefore take unto you the whole armor of God that ye may be able to withstand in the evil day, and having done all, to stand. Stand therefore, having your loins girt about with truth, and having on the breastplate of righteousness; And your feet shod with the preparation of the gospel of peace; Above all, taking the shield of faith, wherewith ye shall be able to quench all the fiery darts of the wicked. And take the helmet of salvation, and the sword of the Spirit, which is the word of God." Ephesians **6:13-18**

There are many good books on Ephesians chapter six. Ask your pastor for a recommendation. I will not focus on the use of these weapons as my emphasis is on the application of scripture as a weapon and a strategy in warfare.

Some of the enemy's dirty tricks are obvious like drugs, alcohol, and the other standard vices. Then there are others that deal with past faults, emotional trauma, disappointments, low self-esteem and the like. Might I suggest that you list all the different ways you have fallen into sin and been tripped up. This will give you the basis for devising a defense.

Of course, your defense is a scripture that contradicts what you feel or think that may be wrong. For example: You have an urge to steal a thing from the store. No one is looking and you are encouraged to swipe it. The defense is, "Thou shalt not steal" Speaking the word out, even in your mind, dispels the evil and keeps you on track. Knowing the scripture to apply in the moment it is needed is the key to victory. That's why you hide it in your heart. (Study it, memorize it and meditate on it)

Strategy In Action... do not be afraid. Stand up and resist the devil with scripture. Use the, "It Is Written" defense to drive him back.

Using A Soft Answer

3. "A soft answer turns away wrath but grievous words stir up anger." Proverbs 15:1

When should you apply this scripture? It wouldn't be in the middle of a sexual temptation. However, it would be just the thing in a knock down battle with your spouse who is the one you supposedly love. Like the scriptures say, "Grievous words stir up strife". The devil knows that if he can get you to spew out words of hate and bitterness that both of you will get hurt.

On the other hand, using a soft answer can be the same as offering an olive branch to an enemy. It suggests to your opponent that you do not want to fight over this issue and are ready to calm down and discuss the matter as mature adults.

What is a soft answer?

A soft answer need not be a weak one, nor should it imply any compromise of truth, nor any yielding of righteousness. It may be firm in substance, though soft in language and spirit.

Very often the most effective reply is given in the mildest tone. It is almost impossible for your adversary to feel bitterness or indignation. When no vital interest of truth or righteousness is at stake, it may be well to yield a point of our own in order to secure peace... [A soft answer] is successful -- not, perhaps, in gaining one's own way, but in turning away wrath. The angry opponent's wrath dies out for lack of fuel.

If you have trouble keeping your cool, remember that one of the fruits of God's Spirit is self-control. Ask Him to fill you with His Spirit so you can be empowered.

Strategy In Action... speak with kindness in your voice and keep away from being angry.

Do Not Be Hasty

4. "Be not hasty in thy spirit to be angry: for anger rests in the bosom of fools." Ecclesiastes 7:9

How you respond to a situation is the key to being victorious. If you jump to conclusions, fly off the handle and react with anger as a defense, you will no doubt escalate the problem and end up looking like a fool. "A prudent *man* foreseeth the evil, and hideth himself: but the simple pass on, and are punished." **Proverbs 22:3**

When I realize that I am angery, A bell, as it were, rings in my spirit indicating that I am on the verge of being a fool or doing a foolish thing. It is hard to acknowledge that you are really a fool because you have allowed anger to take up residence in your soul.

However, it is another snare of the devil to capture you and destroy you. If he can keep anger alive in you, you will eventually self distruct. So when you get angery, be sure to let it pass through you. Do not harbor it for it is the basis for hate, murder, and a bunch of other sick things. Learn to see it in you and reject it at all cost.

All Things Work Together For Good

5. "And we know that all things work together for good to them that love God, to them who are the called according to his purpose." Romans 8:28

Here is a strategy that is sure to work every time. It is, however, predicated on two things: 1.) You must love God. 2.) You must be in the "Them" crowd who are called according to His purposes.

All, "Born Again" folks are in the, "Them" crowd. They make up the church. They are the "Whosoevers" of John 3:16 that believe that Jesus is the Son of God.

All, "Born Again" believers love God. They actually worship Him and adore Him because He first loved us and gave His only Son as a ransom for our souls.

So, do you qualify? If you do, you can rest assured that all things will work together for your good. It may seem like they don't but you do not see the overall picture as God does. He knows the beginning from the end and how to operate around man's free will to cause everything to work out in accordance to His will and in our favor.

We have a clear perspective in **Romans 8:28**. There can be no doubt. What we now are experiencing, good or bad, will ultimately work together for our good. Thus, we can rest when we go through trials and experience tragedies and suffer loss. God is for us and is actively engaged in keeping us in His will and on the right path to Glory.

If you live inside the promise of Romans 8:28, your life is as solid as a rock. Nothing can destroy your peace. However, outside of Romans 8:28 is confusion, hate, fear and anxiety.

Romans 8:28 brings stability and freedom. You simply can't be blown away any more. A sovereign God now governs for your good. He becomes your refuge and source of strength. No promise in all the world is greater than Romans 8:28.

Strategy In Action…rest in the lord, knowing He is in control of your life and destiny.

Defective Weapons Can Not Hurt Us

6. "No weapon formed against you shall prosper, and every tongue *which* rises against you in judgment you shall condemn." Isaiah 54:17

The thought implied is that war comes as the punishment of guilt, and that it is preceded by the "cry" of accusation. Many such cries will rise up against the children of God as they seek to follow their destiny.

We know that the enemy has weapons that are aimed at us. He is poised on the battle field and ready to attack. His fiery darts are made ready and his army is in full battle array. The thing is, his weapons will not prosper because we serve the Lord and walk in the Spirit of the living God.

It's like the enemy is using guns without ammo. He makes a great spectical that can frighten the average person into surrendering his or her authority. But, truth be know, the devil has no power, except that which we surrender to him.

Jesus defeated Satan at every turn. He lived the life we could not live. He died the death we should have died. He rose from the dead and is now the captain of our salvation. Listen to what the scriptures say:

- *"And* having spoiled principalities and powers, he made a shew of them openly, triumphing over them in it." **Colossians 2:15**

- "But God commend his love toward us, in that, while we were yet sinners, Christ died for us." **Romans 5:8**

- Who shall separate us from the love of Christ? *shall* tribulation, or distress, or persecution, or famine, or nakedness, or peril, or sword? As it is written, For thy sake we are killed all the day long; we are accounted as sheep for the slaughter. Nay, in all these things we are more than conquerors through him that loved us. **Romans 8:35-37**

Once you realize that you are more than a conqueror, that nothing can separate you from the love of God, and that Jesus spoiled principalities and powers, you can rest assured that any weapon formed against you will not prosper. It may cause havic and be a bit frustrating but it will not accomplish what it was designed to do. You will make it through and come out on top.

We can comdemn the tounges that wagg in opposition be-
cause we know Jesus has won the victory and we stand in His
accomplishment.

Strategy In Action… to realize that we are fighting a defeated
foe and not to fear his accusations, threats and intimidation.

Three Steps To Success

**7. "Trust in the Lord with all thine heart; and lean not unto
thine own understanding." [6] In all thy ways acknowledge him,
and he shall direct thy paths." Proverbs 3:5-6**

What do you do when you are not sure what to do next? It could
be moving to another state, accepting another job, getting di-
vorced, taking a vacation, experimenting with drugs, giving in
to pre-marital sex, or a host of other decisions that pop up in
everyday life. We seem to be walking in a valley of decisions and
desperately need some answers.

Most of us go to family or co-workers to gain needed advice.
Some seek the counsel of pastors or even therapists. The bottom
line is, "What do we do?" Because we are not sure or just do not
know, Satan will drop answers in our minds so we have a direc-
tion. However, the end of that is death. **Proverbs 14:12** tells us,
"There is a way *that seems* right to a man, but its end *is* the way
of death."

We live in an almost instant society where waiting is outdated. If
we can't get an answer quickly, we seek other sources that will
tell us what they think right away. However, in order to get Godly
counsel and be placed on the right path, we need to Trust In The

Lord with all of our hearts. We also need to acknowledge Him in everything we say and do. **(Proverbs 3:5-6)**

When we trust, we are actually relying upon and adhering to God's Word. Jesus said, "It is written, Man shall not live by bread alone, but by every word that proceeds out of the mouth of God." **Matthew 4:4**

Most folks today live by what the media says, what the pastor says, what the spouse says, and others in their world. It is ok to listen but before we live by what is said, we need to take it before the throne of God and be sure it is actually from God.

We cannot lean to our own understanding. We must listen for the voice of God. He will direct our paths. "Your ears shall hear a word behind you, saying, "This *is* the way, walk in it, whenever you turn to the right hand or whenever you turn to the left." **Isaiah 30:21**

Strategy In Action...Do what the scripture says...Trust! Lean Not! & Acknowledge! Them listen for His voice.

God's Peace Must Rule

8. "And let the peace of God rule in your hearts, to the which also ye are called in one body; and be ye thankful." Colossians 3:15

Here's what Barns Notes say about the Peace of God.

Rule in your hearts - Preside in your hearts; sit as umpire there (Doddridge); govern and control you. The word rendered here "rule" - is commonly used in reference to the Olympic and other games. It means to be a director, or arbiter of the public games; to preside over them and preserve order, and to distribute the prizes to the victors.

The meaning here is, that the peace which God gives to the soul is to be to us what the governor at the games was to those who contended there. It is to preside over and govern the mind; to preserve everything in its place; and to save it from tumult, disorder, and irregularity. The thought is a very beautiful one.

The soul is liable to the agitations of passion and excitement - like an assembled multitude of men. It needs something to preside over it, and keep its various faculties in place and order; and nothing is so well fitted to do this as the calm peace which religion gives, a deep sense of the presence of God, the desire and the evidence of his friendship, the hope of his favor, and the belief that he has forgiven all our sins.

The "peace of God" will thus calm down every agitated element of the soul; subdue the tumult of passion, and preserve the mind in healthful action and order - as a ruler sways and controls the passions of assembled multitudes of people.

Barnes Notes is also good commentary on **Philippians 4:7** that also deals with the peace of God. "And the peace of God, which passes all understanding, shall keep your hearts and minds through Christ Jesus." **Philippians 4:7**

And The Peace of God - The peace that God gives particularly referred to is that which is felt when we have no anxious care about the supply of our needs, and when we go confidently and commit everything into the hands of God. "Thou wilt keep him in perfect peace whose mind is stayed on thee;" **Isaiah 26:3**

Which Passes All Understanding - That is, which surpasses all that people had conceived or imagined. The expression is one that denotes that the peace imparted is of the highest possible kind.

The Christian, committing his way to God, and feeling that he will order all things all right, has a peace which is nowhere else known. No confidence that a man can have in his own powers; no reliance which he can repose on his own plans or on the promises or fidelity of his fellow-men, and no calculations which he can make on the course of events, can impart such peace to the soul as simple confidence in God.

Shall Keep Your Hearts And Minds - That is, shall keep them from anxiety and agitation. The idea is, that by thus making our requests known to God, and going to him in view of all our trials and wants, the mind would be preserved from distressing anxiety. The way to find peace, and to have the heart kept from trouble, is thus to go and spread out all before the Lord. The word rendered here "shall keep," is a military term, and means that the mind would be guarded as a camp or castle is. It would be preserved from the intrusion of anxious fears and alarms.

Through Christ Jesus... It is only in him that the mind can be preserved in peace. It is not by mere confidence in God, or by mere prayer, but it is by confidence in God as he is revealed through the Redeemer, and by faith in him.

Again I say, the moment you feel anxious, fearful, nervous or troubled inside, it is a sure sign that you have lost the peace of God. It's like a referee has blown a whistle and declared you to be off sides. When this happens...when you become aware of it...the thing to do is to seek the Lord, ask forgiveness (Because you have fallen from trusting in God) and ask to be restored.

All the devil needs to do is toss out a thought or mental picture from your past that will cause you to dwell on bad things. His hope is that you will stray from your confidence in God and lose His peace.

Strategy In Action…let the Peace of God referee the actions of your heart.

Angels In Your Midst

9. "The angel of the Lord encamps all around those who fear Him, And delivers them." Psalm 34:7

Picture this…there is a great army of demons in battle array poised to attack you at any moment. You can see their camp-fires everywhere. Suddenly you sense the presence of angels all around you, not just any angels but warring angels. Now they have set up their camp in your midst. The Angel of the Lord, who is the captain of the guard, looks your way and smiles. How does that feel? Probably really great, huh?

Notice the verse that it says the Angel of the Lord not only pro-tects you from approaching danger but also delivers you from harm. The one qualifier in this verse that makes it all happen is you have to be among those who fear or reverence God. If you honor the Lord with your life and substance, His angels are at your disposal. That is a good thing to know when facing evil.

The King James usage of the word, "Fear" is really good because it puts it in perspective. Most Christians, when faced with trou-bling times, complain with some sort of, "Why Me" statement. Their eyes never leave the problem and their voices rehearse the impending doom. However, when we fear God, we are more fo-cused on Him and His awesomeness.

Which is better, to fear what man can do to your or what God can do to you? I'd rather be afraid of displeasing God than worrying about this old world and what it can do to me. It's all about honor and respect for God's authority and right to rule over you. That is what this is all about.

Remember the story in **Matthew 8** of the Centurion that came to Jesus seeking healing for his servant? "The centurion answered and said, Lord, I am not worthy that thou should come under my roof: but speak the word only, and my servant shall be healed." **Matthew 8:8** He respected Jesus' authority and believed that He could but speak the word and things would happen. This is what it means to fear the Lord. You respect, reverence, acknowledge and believe all at the same time. Jesus commented afterwards that He had not seen so great a faith as that of the Centurion.... and the man wasn't even of the house of Israel.

There are a lot of folks I know that complain saying, "Where was God when this or that happened." These same folks rarely spend time in the scriptures to learn His promises and to gain faith. They do not assemble with other believers for Godly fellowship. They do not tithe or even donate to Christian causes. They live in worry, fear and depression. Their faith failed them long ago and all that they can say is, "Where is God?"

These kind of folks have no clue that they are in the battle of the ages and are not aware of warring strategies at their command to defeat the enemy. They will never see the hand of God in their lives nor sense the presence of angels. Don't be like them. Keep your eyes on Jesus and reverence God with your entire being. He will take care of you in hard times.

Strategy In Action...Keep your heart close to God and your conscience clear. Keep your eyes upon the Lord and trust in Him at all times. He will not leave you or forsake you.

Rejoice And Be Glad

10. "This is the day that the Lord has made; let us rejoice and be glad in it." Psalm 118:24

Rejoicing and being glad is the best defense against the devil and his dirty tricks. I will admit that it is hard sometimes to be glad when everything is going wrong in your life. However, the fact that things are getting to you is a sign that you are not where you need to be. *It's all about perspective.*

If you have a right perspective, you can sail right through difficulty, depression and sorrow. Your perspective is what gets you through. It's how you think. If you think negative, you become negative and you feel the pain of all the things that are wrong. If, on the other hand, your perspective is centered in the promises of God, your first thought is to rehearse the scriptures that apply to your difficulty and your prayers are not, "Why Me Lord" but rather, "God will work everything out for my good…so even though I am in a difficulty, He will take care of me." This attitude pulls your spirit up into the faith that is needed to overcome. You are speaking against what you see and feel, declaring what God has said He will do for you.

We can rejoice and be glad because we know that this day, the one we are living in right now, is a day that is especially fashioned for us. It's not just another day. It is a day that the Lord of Glory made. It is full of blessings, wisdom, guidance, joy and faith. That's why we can rejoice and be glad.

The reason folks do not experience this great day is because they don't believe that God would or could create such a day as this for them. They are too busy blaming God for what man has done. It is essential to believe that your everyday is special and God takes great joy in fashioning it just for you.

When you think as I have written, you defeat the devil automatically, without even trying because he cannot dwell in or inhabit your praises to God. That place is reserved only for God. **Psalm 22:3**

Strategy In Action…Jump out of bed tomorrow and shout, "This is the day the lord has made and I will rejoice and be glad in it." Expect good things to happen and refuse to move off that perspective.

Turn On The Light

11. "Thy word is a lamp unto my feet, and a light unto my path" Psalm 119:105

Where do you go when you find yourself in a dark scary place? How do you find your way to daylight and safety? You guessed it, God's Word. It is the lamp that lights the way.

Brown's Bible Commentary says this about Psalm 119:105

"Not only does the Word of God inform us of His will, but, as a light on a path in darkness, it shows us how to follow the right and avoid the wrong way. The lamp of the Word is not the sun. He would blind our eyes in our present fallen state; but we may bless God for the light shining as in a dark place, to guide us until the Son of Righteousness shall come, and we shall be made capable of seeing Him **(2Pe 1:19; Re 22:4)**. The lamp is fed with the oil of the Spirit. The illusion is to the lamps and torches carried at night before an Eastern caravan."

The Word of God is the only true source of wisdom, truth, clarity of right and wrong, attitudinal posture, battle strategies, victory in life and eternity… and so much more. It is our salvation here on this earth and the assurance of salvation beyond this life. It embodies the life and character of Jesus who John, the apostle said was in the beginning with God and was God. **John chapter 1**

God wants us to use His Word to live, move about and have our being. Here are some different references to God's Word.

2Timothy 3:16… "All scripture is given by inspiration of God, and is profitable for doctrine, for reproof, for correction, for instruction in righteousness."

1Thessalonians 2:13 …"For this cause also thank we God without ceasing, because, when ye received the word of God which ye heard of us, ye received *it* not *as* the word of men, but as it is in truth, the word of God, which effectually worketh also in you that believe."

Psalm 119:89 …Forever, O Lord, Thy Word is settled in Heaven.

Isaiah 40:8 … The grass withers, the flower fades: but the word of our God shall stand forever.

Isaiah 55:10,11… For as the rain cometh down, and the snow from heaven, and returns not thither, but waters the earth, and makes it bring forth and bud, that it may give seed to the sower, and bread to the eater: So shall my word be that goes forth out of my mouth: it shall not return unto me void, but it shall accomplish that which I please, and it shall prosper in the thing whereto I sent it.

Matthew 24:35... Heaven and earth shall pass away, but my words shall not pass away.

Psalm 138:2b... Thou hast magnified Thy Word above all Thy name.

John 1:1... In the beginning was the Word, and the Word was with God, and the Word was God.

John 1:14... And the Word was made flesh, and dwelt among us and we beheld his glory, the glory as of the only begotten of the Father, full of grace and truth.

Revelation 19:11-13... And I saw heaven opened, and behold a white horse; and he that sat upon him was called Faithful and True, and in righteousness he doth judge and make war. His eyes were as a flame of fire, and on his head were many crowns; and he had a name written, that no man knew, but he himself. And he was clothed with vesture dipped in blood: and his name is called The Word of God.

Psalm: 33:6 ... By the word of the Lord were the heavens made; and all the host of them by the breath of his mouth.

Hebrews 11:3 ...The worlds were framed by the Word of God.

Ephesians 6:17... The sword of the Spirit, which is the Word of God.

Jeremiah 23:29 ...Is not My Word like as a fire? and like a hammer?

Hebrews 4:12... For the word of God is quick, and powerful, and sharper than any two-edged sword, piercing even to the dividing asunder of soul and spirit, and of the joints and marrow, and is a discerner of the thoughts and intents of the heart.

1John 2:14 …I have written to you, fathers because you have known Him *who is* from the beginning. I have written to you, young men, because you are strong, and the word of God abides in you and you have overcome the wicked one.

James 1:21… Wherefore lay apart all filthiness and superfluity of naughtiness, and receive with meekness the engrafted word, which is able to save your souls. But be ye doers of the word, and not hearers only, deceiving your own selves.

1Peter 1:23… Being born again, not of corruptible seed, but of incorruptible, by the word of God, which lives and abides forever.

Romans 10:17… So then faith cometh by hearing, and hearing by the word of God.

John 15:7… If ye abide in me, and my words abide in you, ye shall ask what ye will, and it shall be done unto you.

John 17:17b… Thy Word is truth.

2Timothy 3:15-17… All Scripture *is* given by inspiration of God, and *is* profitable for doctrine, for reproof, for correction, for instruction in righteousness, that the man of God may be complete, thoroughly equipped for every good work.

Joshua 1:8 …Meditate therein day and night...then shalt thou make thy way prosperous and have good success.

Psalm 119:130…The entrance of Your words gives light; It gives understanding to the simple.

Psalm 119:9… Wherewithal shall a young man cleanse his way? by taking heed thereto according to thy word.

John 15:3… Now ye are clean through the Word, which I have spoken.

Ephesians 5:25-26… Husbands, love your wives, even as Christ also loved the church, and gave himself for it; [26] That he might sanctify and cleanse it with the washing of water by the word;

Psa.107:20… He sent His Word and healed them.

Psalm 119:11… Thy word have I hid in mine heart, that I might not sin against thee.

John 8:31,32… So Jesus said to the Jews who had believed him, "If you abide in my word, you are truly my disciples, [32] and you will know the truth, and the truth will set you free."

1Thessalonian 2:13 …For this cause also thank we God without ceasing, because, when ye received the word of God, which ye heard of us, ye received it not as the word of men, but as it is in truth, the word of God, which effectually works also in you that believe.

8. What we should do with the Word:

Matthew 4:4… "But he answered and said, It is written, Man shall not live by bread alone, but by every word that proceedeth out of the mouth of God."

1Peter 2:2… As newborn babes, desire the sincere milk of Word.

2Timothy 2:15… Study to shew thyself approved unto God, a workman that needs not to be ashamed, rightly dividing the word of truth.

Psalm 119:162… I rejoice at Thy Word, as one that finds great spoil.

Colossians 3:16 … Let the word of Christ dwell in you richly in all wisdom; teaching and admonishing one another in psalms and hymns and spiritual songs, singing with grace in your hearts to the Lord.

Strategy In Action…use the Word to guide you for it will shed light on your path.

Don't Worry, Be Happy

12. "Therefore I tell you, do not worry about your life, what you will eat or drink; or about your body, what you will wear. Is not life more than food, and the body more than clothes?" Matthew 6:25

Worry is defined by the dictionary as, To think about problems or fears: to feel or show fear and concern because you think that something bad has happened or could happen.

How often do you worry? What things do you worry about? Jesus said not to worry about food or clothing but I am sure He means all the other things too, like car payments, sickness, unemployment etc. All of that and more is encapsulated in, **Is not life more than food, and the body more than clothes?** The full aspect of life and happiness is realized, not in worry but in Faith. Worry is the exact opposite of Faith.

Faith is the substance of things hoped for, the evidence of things not seen. **Hebrews 11:1** As you can see, the very nature of faith is to hope for and believe for things not yet seen. Whereas, worry is centered in the fear of loosing what you can see, touch or feel. How many times have I said, I hope I won't loose my job? Or get sick? Or whatever.

Faith will call it forth, knowing that it will come because God spoke it first and declared it to a thousand generations. (As it is written, I have made thee a father of many nations,) before him whom he believed, *even* God, who quickens the dead, and calls those things, which be not as though they were. (**Romans 4:17**) If He will do it for Abraham, He'll do it for us.

When you are afraid and worried, all you need to do is find a promise of God in the Bible. There are over 3,000. Pick the one that fits your situation, knowing that God has spoken it for our benefit. Then ask Him to call it forth for you. You can then do, as Abraham did, repeat it as an act of faith. Doing this will overcome fear and worry because it puts faith back into your spirit and hope that all will be well with your soul.

"Worry is like a rocking chair—it's always in motion but it never gets you anywhere. So why do we struggle with it? And what good does it do? Worry is the opposite of faith, and it steals our peace, physically wears us out, and can even make us sick. When we worry, we torment ourselves—we're doing the devil's job for him! Worry is caused by not trusting God to take care of the various situations in our lives. Too often we trust our own abilities, believing that we can figure out how to take care of our own problems. Yet sometimes, after all our worry and effort to go it alone, we come up short, unable to bring about suitable solutions." Joyce Meyer

*"Historians will probably call our era "the age of anxiety." Anxiety is the natural result when our hopes are centered in anything short of God and His will for us. —**Billy Graham***

Proverbs 29:25 says, "The fear of man brings a snare, but whoever trusts in the Lord shall be safe." This, in my opinion, is the primary cause of worry. We are worried that:

1. People won't like us

2. Someone else is more popular, talented, pretty

3. Others are prospering faster and easier than us

4. Someone will hurt us

5. Our homes will be broken into and our stuff stolen

6. We might be laughed at or put down in some way before others

I am sure you can think of more things that evil men can do to us. However, it's easy to overcome if we put our trust in God and not worry about what man can do to us. God is greater.

Strategy In Action...The best way to overcome Satan's attack using fear, anxiety and worry is to speak out the Word of God, first in your mind and then out loud if need be. Rehearse it over and over until you actually believe it. It will fill your heart with faith and quiet the attack.

The Process

13. "Stand fast therefore in the liberty wherewith Christ hath made us free, and be not entangled again with the yoke of bondage." Galatians 5:1

Anyone that is a true follower of Jesus knows that there is a process that happens. You repent. You receive Jesus as your Savior, You enter the realm of God's grace and you become free of past sins, guilt and all that stuff. You do actually discover the liberty that is in Christ.

The yoke of bondage is removed and you can begin to serve God and be free. The Galatians of the 1st century found this to be true but were bewitched into thinking they had to keep the Law of Moses in order to be a Christian.

The liberty in Christ is God's grace that overcame the law because, as Paul said in another letter, it was weak in the flesh, which means man, could not keep the Law because of his sinful nature. Paul actually rebukes the Galatians in chapter 3-1-3 saying,

"O foolish Galatians, who hath bewitched you, that ye should not obey the truth, before whose eyes Jesus Christ hath been evidently set forth, crucified among you? This only would I learn of you, Received ye the Spirit by the works of the law, or by the hearing of faith? Are ye so foolish, having begun in the Spirit, are ye now made perfect by the flesh?"

The enemy is hard after God's children, ever seeking to get them to make the same mistake as the foolish Galatians. He wants us to operate in the flesh, (our own sinful emotions). Paul tells us what these emotions are in **Chapter 5:19-21,**

" Now the works of the flesh are manifest, which are these; Adultery, fornication, uncleanness, lasciviousness, Idolatry, witchcraft, hatred, variance, emulations, wrath, strife, seditions, heresies, Envyings, murders, drunkenness, revellings, and such like: of the which I tell you before, as I have also told you in time past, that they which do such things shall not inherit the kingdom of God."

We do not want to be foolish and miss out on what God has for us. All these emotions are called, "The Yoke of Bondage." It is what kills us, makes us sick and is displeasing to our Heavenly Father.

We are called into God's grace, which is His unmerited favor. We do not deserve it and yet He gives it to us because we place our faith in Christ.

There are a lot of churches today that believe and teach salvation by works. When you hear that sort of teaching, run for the hills. Here's why:

1. You will be entangled again with its yoke of bondage.

2. It's teaching dishonors the finished work of Christ on the cross.

3. You will always have a question in your spirit of acceptance by God.

4. You will always wonder, "Did I do enough to attain?"

If the do's and don'ts of religion ruled, there would be no need for Christ to go to the cross? His death would have been in vain. It can never by Christ dies for the sins of the whole world but we must still keep the Law. "For by grace are ye saved through faith; and that not of yourselves: it is the gift of God: Not of works, lest any man should boast." **Ephesians 2:8-9**

Strategy In Action… Do not fall for or even entertain the idea that your salvation can be attained by your own efforts. This will stop Satan in his tracts because when you fall short, you can point to Jesus and declare that He won the battle for you and even though you have fallen short, God still loves you.

Saying Thank You Is A Good Practice

14. "In every thing give thanks: for this is the will of God in Christ Jesus concerning you." I Thess. 5:18

The will of God, in Christ, is that you be thankful. Ever wonder why? Because the devil hates those that are thankful to God for what He does in their lives. I can think of several benefits to being thankful or giving thanks. They are:

1. It's a way of overcoming evil with good.

2. It's a call to think positive in every situation.

3. It's a means of spiritual fellowship with the Father God.

4. It's a way of keeping Christ on the throne of your life.

5. It's a show of dependency upon God for life's substance.

6. It's a way of keeping faith alive and active.

7. It's a way to stay in the Spirit and not the flesh.

"Give thanks to the LORD, for he is good; his love endures forever" **1 Chronicles 16:34**

It should be noted that this Bible verse does not say, give thanks **FOR** everything. It says **IN** everything. We would never give thanks to God for a gang rape or murder or terrorist act. We can give thanks in these and other bad events for positive outcomes like survivors or capturing those at fault, etc.

The clear direction given by the verse is to maintain an attitude of thanksgiving in every situation for everything God does in your life. That brings up another theological question.

Does God bring bad things into your life? I have talked to many Christians that actually believe that He does. The misconception comes from a lack of knowledge about God's Sovereign will and man's free will.

God made man with a free will to do what ever he wanted…to be the master of his own life and destiny. God's will was placed second to man's will. It is obvious that man exercised his free will and rebelled against his creator. It is also apparent that we, his descendants, are under the curse of death that God placed upon those who sin. It is also known that God sent Jesus to die for our sins, as a penalty, so we could, if we so desire, rejoin Him in loving fellowship.

With all that said, see the man that lost his child and wife to a drunk driver in a car accident and says, "Why did God allow this to happen?" God didn't revoke Adam's free will to sin and He does not revoke our free will to get drunk, drive and kill others. He does, however say that all of us, everyone both small and great will appears before Him and give an account. Judgment day is right around the corner. **Revelation 20:11**

It was not God but man that caused bad things to happen. Blaming God is the result of an angry erroneous conclusion. "Every good gift and every perfect gift is from above, and cometh down from the Father of lights, with whom is no variableness, neither shadow of turning." **James 1:17**

Giving thanks to God in every situation should be a lifestyle. Imagine if we could practice this principle. There would be no more backbiting, gossip, and no critical attitudes. We would look for the good and perfect gift sent by God and praise Him for His love and grace.

Strategy In Action…In everything, give thanks to God. It will defeat evil forces and keep you in fellowship with your Heavenly Father.

Joy Equals Strength

15. Then he said unto them, "Go your way, eat the fat, and drink the sweet, and send portions unto them for whom nothing is prepared: for this day is holy unto our Lord: neither be ye sorry; for *the joy of the Lord is your strength*." Nehemiah 8:10

This scripture tells us that the Joy of the Lord is our strength. Nehemiah had led the people back from the Babylonian captivity, build the wall around Jerusalem and still they were slaves, in their own minds, to 70 years of bondage. They were free but not inside. They were still without strength.

> When they understood the message of salvation, Nehemiah says, "Then all the people went away to eat and drink, to send portions of food and to celebrate with great joy," *because they now understood the words that had been made known to them.* (8:9-12)

> The *mourning of joy* comes when we realize that we have put our lives together wrong and begin to discover God's instructions on how to take our lives apart and rebuild them.

> When the Word of God is opened up and understood, people begin to understand themselves. It is through knowing God that you begin to come to know yourself. After all you are made in God's image. It is here that you can discover the joy of the Lord as your strength.

The Israelites returned to God and found Him to be a loving Father. They also found Him to be happy, full of Joy that they had repented and returned to him. It is this Joy that keeps us in times of trouble because it comes with the knowledge that God is not mad at us and is actually on our side, working for our good, even if it doesn't seem that way. Thus the Joy of The Lord is our strength.

Strategy In Action…do not beat up on yourself. God has forgiven you so forgive yourself and draw strength from God's joy that you are once again in His loving care…and reject the devil's accusations.

God Is More Important

16. "Delight thyself also in the LORD; and he shall give thee the desires of thine heart." Psalm 37:4

We all have wants and desires that often do not get realized. Satan knows what's going on inside of us. He can see greed, lust and all the things that cause us to want. So, we follow after success, power, fame and riches to provide the desires of our hearts. This process brings sorrow and pain because it is the root of all evil.

Barns Notes commentary offers this explanation…

Delight Thyself Also In The Lord. The word rendered "delight" means properly to live delicately and effeminately; then, to be tender or delicate; then, to live a life of ease or pleasure; then, to find delight or pleasure in anything. The meaning here is, that we should seek our happiness in God - in his being, his perfections, his friendship, his love.

And He Shall Give Thee The Desires of Thine Heart - literally, the "asking," or the "requests" of thy heart. What you really "desire" will be granted to you. That is,

(a) The fact that you seek your happiness in him will regulate your desires, so that you will be "disposed" to ask only those things which it will be proper for him to grant; and

(b) The fact that you do find your happiness in him will be a reason why he will grant your desires.

The fact that a child loves his father, and finds his happiness in doing his will, will do much to regulate his own "wishes" or "desires," and will at the same time be a reason why the father will be disposed to comply with his requests.

The strategy here in overcoming Satan is that when you are so engrossed with the things of God, you will not have time to listen to the accusations and confusion that the devil throws at you. You will automatically dismiss it as foolishness.

Strategy In Action... lose yourself in the things of God and absorb His truths and promises.

Become A Student of The Word

17. "Study to shew thyself approved unto God, a workman that needeth not to be ashamed, rightly dividing the word of truth." II Timothy 2:15

I know what you're about to say, "How can studying be used as a weapon to defeat Satan?" Here are three good reasons:

- Studying the Word of God puts Bible promises at your fingertips for instant recall.

- Studying ushers in wisdom and improves your discernment skills that are needed for spiritual warfare.

- Studying prevents serious mistakes in judgment as you learn a right perspective.

Paul is telling Timothy that he needs to grow in grace and not to go off half-cocked. He must, at all cost, learn the truth, have a clear perspective of life and reality and be able to teach others. The only way to accomplish this is to study.

There was no need to go to college or a trade school. There was no need to sit at the knee of older Christians. Timothy needed to search the scriptures and discover the truths for himself. I can remember my Bible college days. They almost stripped me of my faith. I crammed in 3-years of multiple commentary, selective theology, and dogma only to discover that I didn't know anything about fighting evil forces, rightly dividing the Word of God and it's application in a given situation.

I had to start all over and seek the Lord to form my own perspective. That was over 47 years ago and now I have learned 1st hand by the master teacher, the Lord through His Holy Spirit. Yes, I still listen and read after others but I do not accept anything without searching it out for myself.

How many times have I heard, "My pastor says? Or my church believes?" Folks just do not want to study. It is easier to accept someone else's opinion. That's how folks get led astray…because they do not know the scriptures and therefore cannot discern false teaching.

My wife gets upset with me at times because we will be watching TV, some preacher, and I will holler at the tube, saying, "That's not true." I can spot error right away because I have studied and searched out the truth. I have taken various doctrines before the Lord, questioning them and praying for discernment. I have read and reread scripture passages to find central truths and discover contextual thought.

I am not boasting but trying to show you that being prepared is essential to winning the battle…and it's all about fighting back to keep Satan from stealing God's blessings and our destiny. We cannot let anyone tell us what to think or which doctrine is correct. We must seek it out for ourselves.

Here are a few theological issues to ponder. Can you discern the truth and be prepared to defend it in a discussion with a friend, family member or co-worker that is not a Christian?

1. Which is right, Creation or Evolution? How do you know?

2. Is reincarnation true?

3. Is it ok to have an abortion?

4. Which is correct, salvation by grace or by me being the best person I can be?

5. Does God approve of Gay (Same Sex) Marriage?

6. Drugs, alcohol, free sex and dirty jokes are all ok as long as I do them with moderation, right?

7. Is Christianity the true religion?

These are just a few of life's perplexing questions. What does the Bible say about them? Knowing what God thinks is essential to having a right perspective and overcoming attacks by evil forces.

Strategy In Action…Search it out for yourself and lock it down in your memory so it will be available when Satan comes a calling.

Guard Your Heart

18. "Keep thy heart with all diligence; for out of it *are* the issues of life." Proverbs 4:23

The NIV of this verse says it this way, *"Above all else, guard your heart, for it is the wellspring of life."* It is a little bit clearer. We are to guard our hearts because it is a wellspring of life. It is where life flows and from which we draw strength.

The word, **"Heart"** refers to the inner man. That place where the real you and I exist. It is that being that is judged by God, not our outer appearance. It is our wellspring of life.

The bible has a few things to say about this inner man or heart. Take a read:

1 Samuel 16:7 But the LORD said to Samuel, "Do not look at his appearance or at the height of his stature, because I have rejected him; for God sees not as man sees, for man looks at the outward appearance, but the LORD looks at the heart."

Jeremiah 17:9-10 The heart is more deceitful than all else and is desperately sick; who can understand it? I, the LORD, search the heart; I test the mind, even to give to each man according to his ways, according to the results of his deeds.

These passages teach us that the Lord looks at and searches the heart, the inner person. Why is the heart so important? Because the issues of life—our actions, work, pursuits, etc.—all proceed from the heart (Pr. 4:23; **Matt. 6:21; 12:34; 15:18**). What we do in word and deed is first of all a product of what we are on the inside.

The problem with our heart or inner man is that it trusts in itself as a source of reasoning and solutions. We were created to be dependant upon God and for Him to be our source. It was the bond of unity that brought man and God together as one.

Jeremiah saw the inner man as full of deceit and desperately wicked. Paul, the Apostle also saw man this way when he said, "As it is written, There is none righteous, no, not one:" **Romans 3:10**

The heart is our mind, will and emotions. It is where we live and move and have our being. If we choose to allow unbelief to rule our heart, we miss out on all the blessings and favor of God. We remain unregenerate and depraved, without hope in a world dominated by sin.

There is no neutral ground. We are either isolated from God, dead in our sins and alone to face life's many trials or we are empowered by God's Spirit, renewed in the inner man, full of faith and trust in God that He will direct our steps in life and keep us from evil.

God says this through Ezekiel, "A new heart also will I give you, and a new spirit will I put within you: and I will take away the stony heart out of your flesh, and I will give you an heart of flesh." **Ezekiel 36:26**

This is the essence of being, "Born Again." Being born again unites us with God the Father through our faith in Christ and fills our heart (Mind Will & Emotions) with the Spirit of the living

God. Remember what the Word says, "For God hath not given us the spirit of fear; but of power, and of love, and of a sound mind." **II Timothy1:7**

Satan will try to keep you in fear and confusion but if we put on the new man, which after God, is created in righteousness and true holiness." **Ephesians 4:24,** we need not worry, fret, fear or have any anxiety in life's daily walk. It is this that we are to guard, so we do not let it slip away. It is here, out of the new heart that life springs up with the issues of life, God's life.

For those who were there and somehow have lost it, I have this word for you from God. "Draw nigh to God, and he will draw nigh to you. Cleanse your hands, ye sinners; and purify your hearts, ye double minded." **James 4:8**

"Trust in the Lord with all thine heart; and lean not unto thine own understanding. In all thy ways acknowledge him, and he shall direct thy paths." **Proverbs 3:5-6**

If you missed the point, here it is in plain talk. Go back to the Lord; ask forgiveness for your unbelief. You are where you are because you stopped believing. You will have to fight the fear, the worry, the devil and anything else with the scriptures until they become alive in you again. Fight the good fight of faith until you are on top once again.

Strategy In Action…Hang on to the scriptures, apply them and believe them with your whole heart.

The Bible Is The Final Authority

19. "All scripture _is_ given by inspiration of God, and _is_ profit-

able for doctrine, for reproof, for correction, for instruction in righteousness" II Timothy 3:16

I have used the Bible as my final authority to share this book with you. **II Timothy 3:16** is why. It is the inspired Word of God and is profitable for reproof, correction and instruction in righteousness. It is the Sword of the Spirit and can easily bring you back to God, fill you with faith, educate you in Spiritual Warfare, deliver you from demons and keep your heart in peace.

When you use it against Satan, he has no recourse. He has to submit to its authority because it is the Living Word of God. Using it as your source, as a governing rule of practice, is the best way to gain and maintain victory. Hide it in your heart and use it in every situation.

Strategy In Action…Stay in the scriptures and live by the truths it proclaims.

There Is Only One Way

20. "Jesus said to him, "I am the way, and the truth, and the life; no one comes to the Father but through Me." John 14:6

It is hard for most folks that are not "Born Again" to understand why there is just one way to God, yet it is true. There is only one way and that is through Jesus Christ. The Bible is our source to prove that the one-way doctrine is valid. **Acts 4:12** says, "Neither is there salvation in any other: for there is none other name under heaven given among men, whereby we must be saved."

Jesus is the only way to attain salvation. All the world religions cannot save us. Joining a church or specific faith cannot save us. It must be an acknowledgment of our sin, our cry before the throne of God for forgiveness, and our invitation for Jesus to come into our hearts and save us. His name is the only one that can get us through death into eternal life.

Here are a few scriptures that support the only "One-Way" doctrine.

- ...there is one God, and one mediator between God and men, the man Christ Jesus; Who gave himself a ransom for all, to be testified in due time. **(I Timothy 2:5-6)**

- ...Believe on the Lord Jesus Christ and thou shalt be saved... **(Acts 16:31)**

- That if thou shalt confess with thy mouth the Lord Jesus, and shalt believe in thine heart that God hath raised him from the dead, THOU SHALT BE SAVED. For with the heart man believeth unto righteousness; and with the mouth confession is made unto salvation. **(Romans 10:9-10)**

The skeptic would say, "You mean to tell me that all the religions of the world are wrong and only Christianity is the one true religion?" Remember, Christianity is not a religion. It is a relationship born out of love between man and the one true and living God.

There is no one true religion. Religion, in itself, will not get us to God. It is the blood of Christ that unlocks the door and our confession of faith in Jesus that makes it all happen. **(John 14:6)**

Why is Jesus the only way to God? He is the only way because God planned it that way. He set the penalty for sin, which was death. *The soul that sinneth, it shall die.* **(Ezekiel 18:20)** In fact,

Jesus was the slain Lamb of God before the foundation of the world. **(Ephesians 1:3-7)**

Jesus Himself said, as recorded in **John 14:6,** "I am the way, the truth, and the life: No man cometh to the Father but by Me." Christianity states that the God of the Bible is the only true God and salvation is only possible by accepting Jesus Christ, His only begotten Son as Savior and Lord. **II Corinthians 5:21** says, "For he hath made him to be sin for us, who knew no sin; that we might be made the righteousness of God in him."

God validated His Son as the only way in multiple ways so we could be assured that Jesus was indeed the only way to Him. Here are some to consider.

1. He claimed to be the only way as in **John's record 14:6** says but validation came through miracles that proved He was who He claimed to be.

2. Eyewitnesses saw Jesus' miracles and validated them as authentic. Over 500 followers saw Jesus, after His resurrection, and watched Him ascend into heaven.

3. The prophets foretold of His coming, where He would be born, that He would be God in human flesh and lots more...all prophetic statements were realized in Jesus, even those like in Isaiah chapter 53 that were uttered hundreds of years before Jesus came.

4. God Himself validated Jesus as His sole pathway to Him. "While he was still speaking, behold, a bright cloud overshadowed them; and suddenly a voice came out of the cloud, saying, "This is My beloved Son, in

whom I am well pleased. Hear ye Him!"**(Mathew 17:5)**

5. The Apostles lost their homes, wealth, and even their lives preaching the gospel. Would they do that if it were a lie? I don't think so. They testified to the truth and were willing to die for it if necessary. (See Foxes Book of Martyrs)

6. Thousands of Believers, over several centuries have testified of how Jesus helped them and blessed them.

7. I can personally testify that I have seen the hand of the Lord in my life and communicate with Him daily. I know He is the Christ.

The provability that one man could fulfill all prophecies about a Messiah that God Himself said would come, **(Gen.3:15),** and perform fantastic miracles while here on earth, and be raised from the dead, and ascend into heaven while hundreds looked on is astronomical. But Jesus did just that…fulfilled everything that was foretold about the coming Messiah. He had to be who He said He was and therefore is truly the only way to God.

Strategy In Action…Believe in Jesus because He is the only way we can live here and attain eternity.

PART IV HAVING DOMINION

So far, we have discussed the battle, the battleground, the two opposing forces, the weapons of our warfare, the battle strategies, the believer's authority and shown examples of practical applications to attain victory. In part IV we will discuss having dominion.

The psalmist said, "Blessed be the LORD my strength which teaches my hands to war, and my fingers to fight: my goodness, and my fortress; my high tower, and my deliverer; my shield, and he in whom I trust; who subdueth my people under me." Psalm 144:1-3

God wants His children to participate in the battle. That's why all the armor, strategies and counsel. It is to accomplish His original command to man when he was created.

We can see that one of the purposes of man's existence and why he was made in the image of God. is to "have dominion over the fish of the sea, and over the birds of the air, and over the cattle, and over all the wild animals of the earth, and over every creeping thing that creeps upon the earth" (**Gen. 1:26**) I am sure you are aware that the devil took the form of a snake in the deception of Eve.

We are to have dominion. That means to use all we have learned from being with the Lord to stop the devil's influence upon the earth. I know that seems way too big for little old you and me. However, the church could accomplish it if it came together. All we have to do is get more than 3,000 different denominations and Christian groups to come together in an, upper room, as it were and come into one accord.

Since that would be most unlikely, the dominion will be limited to our world, as small or big as it is. We can still have dominion over the things that affect us in the life. Having dominion is to become the authority, the head decision maker. However, all decisions are routed through the Holy Spirit before implementation. We do not go off half-cocked to fight in our own flesh. Remember, the battle is the Lord's. We are to do what the Bible says:

1. **Stand fast** therefore in the *liberty* wherewith Christ hath made us free, and be not entangled again with the yoke of bondage. Galatians 5:1

2. **Watch** ye, stand fast in the faith, quit you like men, and be strong. Let all your things be done with charity. I Corinthians 16:3-4

3. **Be sober**, be vigilant; because your adversary the devil, as a roaring lion, walks about, seeking whom he may devour: Whom **resist** stedfast in the faith, knowing that the same afflictions are accomplished in your brethren that are in the world.

4. Finally, my brethren, **be strong** in the Lord, and in the power of his might. Ephesians 6:12

Dominion And Authority

The difference between dominion and authority is that dominion is power or the use of power; sovereignty over something; stewardship, supremacy. Authority is the power to enforce rules or give orders. We, in the name of Jesus, have been endowed with both through the Holy Spirit. We hold the position and are able to enforce the rules by our, "Free Will" decisions. We speak the promises of God power our lives and our loved ones.

Understanding dominion is crucial to walking with God. A lack of understanding can lead to defeat in the time of battle. Spiritual dominion is always a delegated power granted by God. It is only effective when we're totally submitted to the will of God. You cannot go around commanding spirits or people at you pleasure. You can, however, speak the word with authority over a situation or against an evil spirit. Jesus did this when being tempted in the wilderness. He said, "It is written." We can do the same, knowing He will honor His word.

Dominion is about knowing who you are in Christ. It is understanding that in you, through Him can possess the promises of God. It is also about knowing that you can do what God said you can do, have what God said you can have and be what God said you can be.

Walking in a posture of dominion involves serious commitment; A keen knowledge that the, "Flesh" is your greatest enemy and realizing that God's word remains true no matter what is going on. It is remaining steadfast in your faith; Staying in control of your emotions; and staying in an attitude of worship and praise.

The ultimate goal of taking dominion is to bring glory to God.

Everything should be done with one single purpose- to glorify the name of Jesus in the earth.

We cannot subdue and rule over anything apart from our Savior's power. "Apart from him, we can do nothing." <u>John 15:5</u>. However, we have been endowed with His power by His own Spirit. "For God hath *not given* us the *spirit of fear*; but of power, and of love, and of a sound mind." 2 Timothy 1:7

CONCLUSION

All of the teaching presented here is to overcome the wilds or tricks of the devil. Some will say that I make too much of a battle with evil and that I ought to focus my teachings on more positive things. If I don't educate you as to the enemy and show you how to overcome, you will be the most defeated Christian in our times.

That is what we have today, bless me Christians who are not even sure that there is an enemy bent on their destruction. Believe me, there is a real devil and he will stop at nothing. He works night and day to scheme and plot ways to steal your joy, kill your dreams and destroy your destiny.

It is crazy to say I can stay neutral or that there is no devil. These are the last days before the return of Christ. He will soon come to earth and we will see Him in the clouds of heaven with all His angels.

However, we are now in a life and death struggle for our own souls. The scriptures I have shared are not all there is. I am sure you will find more as you search the Word of God. They are meant to get you started and keep you safe as a victorious Christian that need not to be ashamed.

May our Lord bless you and keep you. May His face shine upon you and give you peace.

SELECTED CHRISTIAN POETRY BY JOHN MARINELLI, THE AUTHOR

"I AM" There

"I AM" There,
At the end of your broken dreams,
Before the sun rises over your day,
Prior to those tear-filled streams.

"I AM" There,
Down that road of despair,
When all appears to be lost,
And no one seems to care.

"I AM" There,
Over all of life's twists and turns,
When tomorrow is all but gone,
And when you are full of concerns.

"**I AM**" There,
Sayeth the Lord of Host,
To bring you hope and peace,
And the power of my Holy Ghost.

"**I AM**" There,
To be sure you make it through,
In the midst of every trial,
To bless your life and deliver you.

"I Am" There

"All power is given unto me in heaven and earth. Go ye therefore and teach all nations, baptizing them in the name of the Father, and of the Son, and of the Holy Ghost: Teaching them to observe all things, whatsoever I have commanded you: and lo, I am with you always, even unto the end of the world." Mathew 28:18-20

The Lord is with us always. He never leaves our side, even when we leave His. In every situation, He is there. It's time to count on His presence and trust in His grace.

Guardian Angel

The Angel of the Lord
Comes with a mighty army,
To fight the enemies of God.

Then he opens our eyes
That we might see the battle
And walk where angels trod.

Our guardian angels
Beholds the very face of God,
Standing there on our behalf.

Our guardian angels
Are ready with God's power,
To quiet evil's awful wrath.

"Take heed that ye despise not one of these little ones; for I say unto you, That in heaven, there angels do always behold the face of my Father, which is in heaven" Mathew 18:10

As God's children, we have guardian angels that watch over us and report back to God. They are ministering spirits especially placed in service to help the saints on their way to glory.

The Angel's Camp

The angel of the Lord
Sets up his camp
Around those that reverence God.

Imagine being there
In the midst of
Where angels trod.

What a joy it is
To know God's protection
And to be in the angel's camp.

It is there that God's children
Are delivered from evil's woe
And led by heaven's lamp.

" The angel of the Lord encamps round about them that fear Him, and delivers them" Psalm 34:7

Deliverance come through reverence and respect for God and a belief that He will be there with His angels to help you in times of trouble.

All Creation Waits

A blue-gray sky
Winks at the dawn,
As the morning light
Sings its glorious song.

Life is flourishing everywhere,
Unaware of what's in store.
The sounds of spring beckons,
In a silent and peaceful roar.

Time marches onward,
Towards the brink of day,
As all of creation waits
For God's children to pray.

It's time to stand up and be counted as a child of God. It's time to pray for peace and deliverance. Creation is waiting.

Don't Worry

Don't worry about tomorrow.
You did that yesterday.
Go on with your life
And remember always to pray.

Ask and it shall be given to you,
But this great truth you already know.
Rejoice and be happy, why? Because…
Your harvest comes from what you sow.

I will say it again and even more,
Until it becomes very very clear.
Tomorrow will take care of itself,
But worry is another word for fear.

Now here's what I want you to do.
Trust in the Lord and be of good cheer.
Drop the worry from your vocabulary
And cast out that demon of fear.

Worry is a sin so stop it. Be of good cheer. It's all up to you. Life
is too short to spend it worrying.

Arm's Length

I hold the world at arm's length,
That its choices do not interfere.
While it does its own thing,
I watch and wait over here.

My steps must not go that way,
For it's not where I need to be.
The Lord has shown me the path,
That will lead me to my destiny.

The call to follow sin is strong
And pulls at me now and then.
But I know that way
Is full of sorrow and sin.

I must move on in life
Beyond their beckoning call.
It's the right thing to do,
So I do not stumble or fall.

I will not be swayed or misled
By family, friends or business deal.
Their secret thoughts are not mine,
To consider, to admire or feel.

So I keep the world at "Arm's Length"
As I journey through this life.
My faith in Jesus keeps me strong,
As I walk in His glorious light.

Arm's length is a good policy. Be sure you stay in the Lord and close to Him. It's the only way to keep sane in such a crazy world.

Clutter

Clutter keeps the mind confused,
As images dance through the night.
Lost among those unimportant thoughts,
Are the dreams that once shined bright.

An endless parade of fear and doubt,
Crowds the mind to destroy our day.
Ever soaring on the wings of the soul,
Until it has formed an evil array.

But clutter is by one's choice,
Of those who dance to its beat.
Better to face imaginations' due
Than to fall into utter defeat.

Set up a filter that keeps out unnecessary thoughts. A good practice is to go by the still waters in your mind and rest there until the flow of life situations becomes manageable.

I Find Myself In God

I find myself in God.
He is my "everything"
I know that He is Lord,
My Life, my Hope, and King.

I find myself in God,
Not the ways of sin.
Nor do I look to others,
To know who I really am.

I find myself in God,
To whom I bow on bended knee.
He alone is my joy and strength
And where I want to be.

You cannot really know yourself unless you first know God. He created you in His images and until you discover Him, you will never find yourself.

The Angels Cry "Holy,"

The Angels cry "Holy,"
While sorrow fills the land.
For God's Judgment Day,
Is to come upon every man.

The Angels cry "Holy,"
While mankind goes astray,
Rejecting the love of God,
To follow his own precarious way.

The Angels cry "Holy,"
Knowing the terror of the Lord,
When all who dwell in sin,
Will suddenly be destroyed.

The Angels cry "Holy,"
Waiting for all things new,
Born of the Holy Spirit,
When God's Judgment is through.

The Angels cry "Holy,"
"Holy is the Lamb,"

Waiting for the children of God,
To join "The Great I AM"

Heaven is waiting for us to join our Savior. What a great day that will be. Are you ready? I am.

Rest My Child

Take your peace and be restored
Then put your faith in Jesus, the Lord
He has provided, your mouth to feed.
From the beginning, He knew your need.

Do not worry, fret or even fear,
for, my child, He is always near.
To bless your soul with love and grace,
To be with you, face to face.

Come, my child, near to His throne.
Do not allow your faith to roam.
For those who will not believe,
Can never find rest in times of need.

His word shall see you through.
His grace He freely gives to you.
That you should rest, your soul to keep,
Forever delivered from unbelief.

Go ahead, rest in the Lord. I dare you. It may be scary at first but it sure feels good when you get use to it.

Winning The Battle

We must use the Word of God
To calm emotions that fray.
For the enemy never sleeps,
Until he has led us astray.

So when your emotions overflow
With feelings like depression and fear.
Know this! If you dwell in that place,
You invite the enemy to draw near.

When your emotions rage
With fiery darts aglow,
Stand in the power of the Lord,
Against its awful woe.

And if you get confused
And lost in the storm,
Put your thoughts on trial,
Rejecting all but heaven born.

You can win the battle
That rages within your soul.
By casting down imaginations,
And breaking Satan's hold.

Remember to focus on Jesus,
Holding the world at arm's length.
Lift up your head above the trial,
And the Lord will give you strength.

"For the weapons of our warfare are not carnal but mighty, through God, to the pulling down of strongholds: casting down imaginations and every high thing that exalts itself against the knowledge of God, and bringing into captivity every thought to the obedience of Christ." II Corinthians 10:3-5 The battle is in our minds and we win by putting our thoughts on trial and casting out all that oppose the knowledge of God. This is true victory.

Little Prisons

Little prisons await the man with a lustful soul.
Bars of selfishness and pride create dungeons of icy cold.

Prisons of shame and jealousy fill the heart with utter despair.
Bars that separate from God and those that really care.

Stand back! While the doors are tightly closed;
Taking away your life, to wither as a dying rose.

Beware of those little prisons that trap the lustful soul.
Keep yourself free from sin through faith in the Christ of old.

Little prisons need not to be your fate.
It is your choice, Spirit or flesh to date.

"O Foolish Galatians, who hath bewitched you, that ye should not obey the truth, before whose eyes Jesus Christ hath been, evidently set forth, crucified among you? Are you so foolish? Having begun in the Spirit, are you now made perfect in the flesh?

We should always seek to dwell in the Spirit, that we would not emulate the deeds of the flesh. When we fall short, we create "little prisons" that keep us in confusion and away from the blessing of God. It's time to walk in the Spirit and break the prisons that so easily beset us

The Wrestling Match

We wrestle not with flesh and blood,
For man is not our enemy.
Instead, we fight demons in the spirit
That seek to steal our destiny.

But our weapons are not earthly,
Like tanks, guns or bombs.
Instead, we "Plead The Blood"
And shout our victory songs.

So do not wrestle with humanity
Even though evil is there.
Go after Satan, the real enemy
And strip his kingdom bare.

"For though we walk in the flesh, we do not war after the flesh: for the weapons of our warfare are not carnal but mighty, through God, to the pulling down of strongholds; casting down imaginations and every high thing that exalts itself above the knowledge of God, and bring into captivity, every thought to the obedience of Christ." II Corinthians 10: 3-6

Don't fight with other people. Just go about your own business, counting on God to be the avenger. He is the one that holds all the power and strength. If we fight in the flesh, we can fall to strongholds and demons. But standing up in the Spirit and using the name of Jesus, applying the knowledge of God in the situation and casting down every ungodly imagination, will always lead us to victory.

Oh' The Blood

Oh, the blood of Jesus
That washed away my sin.
What a great blessing
To have God as my friend.

This one thing I know for sure,
That when I confess my sin,
His cleansing blood will flow,
And I can walk again with Him.

Oh, the blood of Jesus,
How great a sacrifice for me.
For it was the blood of the Lamb
That healed my soul and set me free.

"If we confess our sins, he is faithful and just to forgive us our sins and to cleanse us from all unrighteousness." I John 1:9

It is the blood of Jesus that is the cleansing agent in forgiveness, acceptance by God and salvation of the soul. Without His blood, there would be no payment for sin. Saint John, in chapter three, says that the wages for sin is death. Jesus paid the price so we could go free to serve God, the Father.

One Man

It was by one man, Adam,
That the world fell into sin.
He chose to disobey God's word
And lost God's Spirit within.

No more walks with God
Through the garden of God's grace.
No more close up and personal
To walk along and talk, face to face.

One man, Adam, gave up
The very nature of God.
Never again to stroll along
Where angels once trod.

Evil now flows through his blood
Where only righteousness was before.
He gave up the Spirit of life
To open up death's awful door.

But one Man, Jesus, came from God
To seek and to save that which was lost.
The life of God in man, once again,
Because He paid sin's incredible cost.

" Therefore, as by one man, sin entered into the world, and death by sin; and so death passed upon all men, for that all have sinned. For as by one man's disobedience, many were made sinners, so by the obedience of one, many shall be made righteous." Romans 5:12 & 19

Adam fell and lost the Spirit of God inside of him because of his disobedience; But Jesus obeyed, did not fall and restored what Adam lost. All die in Adam because of sin but all who believe in Jesus shall live in Christ because of His righteousness.

In The Fullness of Time

In the fullness of time,
Jesus came, made of a woman.
Our Heavenly Father sent Him
Because our adoption was at hand.

He was born under the law,
So He might redeem us from it,
And to receive adoption as sons,
Being children of God, we sit.

We who God made His children,
Have the Spirit of His Son,
Deep within our heart of hearts,
So we can finally become one.

"But when the fullness of time was come, God sent forth his son, made of a woman, made under the law, to redeem them that were under the law, that we might receive the adoption of sons. And because we are sons, God has sent forth the spirit of his son into our hearts, crying, Abba, Father." Galatians 4:4-6

We are the adopted sons of God. We, like no other, have the indwelling presence of the Spirit of His Son, who cries out unto God the Father. If your spirit is not crying out to God, you may want to find out why?

Fragile Flower Red

As a flower in earthen sod,
I bloom for thee, oh God.
To blossom with the turn of spring;
To be to you, a beautiful thing.

I lift my Fragile Flower Red
Upward from my earthen bed;
To draw light from God above,
Strength and peace and joy and love.

As a flower, I bloom for thee
That passersby may stop and see.
Your fragrance and beauty I am,
Flowered in grace as a man.

As a flower in earthen sod,
I bloom for thee, oh God.
Upward, I lift my head,
As a Fragile Flower Red.

"Be not conformed to this world, but be ye transformed, by the renewing of your mind, that ye may prove what is that good and acceptable and perfect will of God."

When we look to God as our source, we blossom, much like a

flower that draws light from the sun. When we blossom, like a flower, we display the glory and beauty of our creator to all who care to stop and look. This is our divine providence.

ABOUT THE AUTHOR

John Marinelli

Rev. Marinelli is an ordained Christian minister. John is the author of several other books, "The Art of Writing Christian Poetry", "Original Story Poems," a children's book, "Mysteries & Miracles," "Moonlight & Mistletoe", "With Eagle's Wings" which are Christian Fiction stories and "Pulpit Poems," a collection of over 250 Christian Poems for use by Pastors and teachers. (www.christianliferesourcecenter.org)

John has authored several one act plays and monologues that were marketed through Russell House Publishing to churches nationwide for use in their performance ministries. He is also a dedicated Christian poet with award winning poems, some of which are permanently displayed on 3' X 4'billboards in Holy

Land USA, a 250 acre nature park in Bedford, VA. Several other poems are framed and displayed at the Christian Church Conference Center is Silver Springs, Florida.

He has appeared with his wife, Marilyn on several TV programs including Trinity Broadcasting Network in Jacksonville Beach and Miami, Florida, as well as, numerous radio station interviews around the country.

He is now retired and living in central Florida where he continues to write and publish Christian related books.

CPSIA information can be obtained
at www.ICGtesting.com
Printed in the USA
BVHW031217100221
599800BV00002B/108